Horse *as* Teacher

The Path to Relationship

Linda-Ann Bowling
Rachel Dexheimer
Juli Lynch
Vanessa Malvicini
Mary Elizabeth Meyers
Caroline Rider
Helen Amanda Russell
Debra A. Saum
Sandra Wallin
Birgit Weskamp

Kathy Pike and Marilyn Schwader, Editors

CLARITY OF VISION PUBLISHING • PORTLAND, OREGON

Also Available: Horse as Teacher: The Path to Authenticity

For more information, visit www.HorseAsTeacher.com

BOOK DESIGN AND PRODUCTION BY MARILYN SCHWADER
COVER PHOTO BY SUSAN WILLIAMS, WWW.WINDHORSEONE.COM
CO-EDITORS: KATHY PIKE AND MARILYN SCHWADER

ISBN: 978-0-9824494-1-7
Library of Congress Control Number: 2009939342

Table of Contents

Foreword

The collaborative authors in the *Horse as Teacher* series have done it again! The appeal of these stories from persistent, patient women who both teach and learn with the help of horses, is in their authentic voices. Listening to and allowing the expression of the healing gifts horses offer through relationship deepens awareness and develops consciousness. This collection of stories offers us the opportunity to step into that world and experience what horses can teach us about relationship.

The sheer breadth, depth, and scope of these *Horse as Teacher* stories carry "high tear factor", words used by one of my students to describe really moving, exceptionally authentic, quality crafted work. Through this work, I discovered bits and pieces of myself in these wonderful accounts of insight development and personal growth.

The authors represent varied traditions and disciplines, and through the writing, I learned different ways of being with horse. In the opening of Sandra Wallin's very moving story, *A Grace Remembered,* Wayne Dyer is quoted: "When you change the way you look at things, the things you look at change." A shift in perception is the thread that weaves its way through these chapters as the authors describe their relationship with horse(s).

Horses have been attempting to reach and teach me all my life. Nearly seven decades ago, as a youthful seven year-old girl spending time with my maternal grandmother, I was introduced to the Mexican ponies and burros she had acquired "across the line" from Douglas, Arizona. I played Indian Princess and Desert Scout Tracker with my brother Walt, sister Susan, and the neighborhood gang.

Every year until I started school at the University of Tucson, Susan, Walt, and I stayed with my aunt, Sister Agnes Wager. She knew a family from Agua Prieta, Mexico who lent us three burros for the duration of our visits. When our time in Arizona ended, Floppy, Elmer, and Daisy would stay in Mexico during the nine months we lived away in Cleveland, Ohio.

I know now that the privilege of learning the language of Equus from these strong-willed, independent burros living in our back yard gave me skills with horses that I didn't appreciate until many years later as a three day event rider, and now a dressage enthusiast.

Back then, there were no saddles, halters, bareback pads, or bridles. We rode them as their Mexican family did, with a stick pointing the way. A certain famous natural horseman has made much money teaching folks what is actually a very ancient way with horses. The idea of haltering and leading Floppy – Her Self, my childhood companion and mate, makes me smile. The whole scene was ludicrous, really, as she required me to approach her, make friends, coo and hum with obvious affection for her marvelous self, hand massage her dense stiff all-weather coat, rub her back and up behind her surprisingly soft and communicative ears, and finally offer treats of apples or carrots.

If no one was around to give me a leg up and hand me the stick, then I would "imaginary lead line – companion walk" her over to the kitchen step to stand sideways and quiet, while I carefully slid my leg over. I practiced great caution in keeping the stick very still, so as to not unintentionally signal a go forward or turn. I learned experientially, through doing, how gravity truly held me balanced astride her ridged back. And yes, I took many dusty plops onto the dry desert sands. And no, there were no hard hats in the vicinity.

When burros are done with adventuring, they are done. They put their heads down and start to eat. You can attempt to urge them forward and sometimes – very rarely – that works. Frequently, the next best step was to lie back and cloud gaze to wait for her to go home. Sometimes, frustrated, I would slide off and head home. She always followed me.

What lesson of attachment, relationship bonding, and horse/human communication was I absorbing from Floppy, Elmer, and Daisy? Floppy as lead mare was always mine, the older sister charged with looking after Walt and Susan. What guided them to choose each of us as they so clearly did, year after year?

Answers to these questions and other mysteries of relationship lie within the pages of this rich, resourceful book. Be ready to see relationships in a whole new way.

Barbara K. Rector, MA, CEIP-ED
Director, Adventures In Awareness
www.adventuresinawareness.net

Preface

Watch a herd of horses and you will see the power of collective group consciousness. One horse grazes while another is scanning the horizon following the subtle scent of a predator, determining if the group needs to seek safety. The lead mare uses her innate sixth sense to find the next water hole. When an imminent storm is brewing miles away, another is keen on finding good shelter. Meanwhile others enjoy mutually satisfying grooming or are engaging in expressive play – a highly intellectual form of animal behavior. Each individual within the herd contributes to the collective with their innate talents. Time is freed up and the herd thrives from the support provided by each other.

Far away on a mountain range is a single horse, solo and elusive. The horse is in hyper awareness, only allowing for extremely short breaks of sleep. Who would warn him of the mountain lion encroaching in his space if he goes into a deep slumber? While he drinks from the stream, he keeps a constant look in all directions. Once his drink is complete he quickly focuses on finding food. An endless array of responsibilities consume his every moment; there is no time for play and relaxing. So focused on surviving, he lacks the strength and resources to find his own mare, to begin his own herd, to thrive in the natural process of a wild animal.

Many years ago I was the solo horse. Surviving. I was completely unaware of it because I had known no other way. As a single woman and entrepreneur, I was used to getting it all done and relying only on myself. I was building my business and yet, personally, deeply alone, exhausted with the constant work and no energy left for play or to find a mate. Somewhere and some how I had accepted this as my way of life.

Then horses came into my life again. I did not seek them, rather they found me. They arrived in my life and offered their kinship. Without hesitation I allowed them in. It was not until I began to understand the "way of the horse" that I learned a new way of being, a new way of connecting, a way that led me from lonely self-sufficiency to collaborative, co-creating partnerships that offered greater levels of comfort, safety, and expansion.

It hasn't always been easy, pretty, or perfect. I shared in the first *Horse as Teacher* book a story about Corazon, the wild horse from the Pryor Mountain Range. He taught me the power of listening in relationships and how to take a deep look at the shadowy sides of my personality that he wanted nothing to do with. In my book *Hope. . . from the Heart of Horses* I share personal and client stories of the strife and rewards of the human and horse interaction, the process of developing a relationship that is based on shared respect and understanding.

The turning point of my consciousness was when I began to see everything the horses offered me as a form of communication, not only about their needs, but as a reflection of who I am in the relationship. It was obvious I could not and did not want to dominate or use force as part of the process. Then what was left? Listening, connecting, and seeking to understand, first and foremost, was what I discovered. Any relationship is a two way street and the horses taught me how to collaborate with them, to honor their strengths, and have patience when they struggled to understand.

Many things in my life changed once horses became an integral part of my daily experience. I truly comprehended the depth of my exhausted way of life. I was functioning like the solo horse out on the range.

I began to apply the teachings from the horses, the power of a herd, into my human world. I saw that to be fully who I was meant to be, I would need to have my own herd, to have a sense of belonging and to be willing to empower others in their innate talents. Slowly, I drew to me many amazing and generous healers who helped with programs and in the building of the Equine Facilitated Learning and Coaching field. The more I honored their talents and trusted them in working with me, the more we all grew.

It was the emergence of the *Horse as Teacher* project that took my understanding of the strength of a herd to a completely new level. Through developing the *Horse As Teacher* books, each one including many wonderful teachers offering pearls of wisdom, that suddenly my world began to flourish. The authors have become a herd, a collective of wisdom, each offering what is most meaningful to them. Together, with the power of many, they are ready to influence and shape the consciousness that is now being held around the meaning of horses and the meaning of relationships in our lives at this point in societies' evolution.

It is a great honor to be a co-founder of this project, and to believe in so many women, offering them a place to have a voice and to move from

from being solo entrepreneurs into being a part of a powerful collective of caring women wanting to offer the world new points of views and ways of being.

These women, some of them splashy paints or subtle bays; others with dashing manes and tails; some with tall regal necks; others with robust presence and strength; most of them lead mares with the energy of a stallion, all full of wisdom and grace, offer their stories to expand your mind and encourage you to explore your view of the horse as teacher.

Kathy Pike, Co-Editor
Co-Founder of Horse as Teacher
www.coachingwithhorses.com

A Grace Remembered

By Sandra Wallin

"When you change the way you look at things, the things you look at change." I first heard these words from Wayne Dyer while watching one of his PBS specials, but their significance became clear only after Grace came into my life…

Grace and I met in 2003 at one of Linda Kohanov's Epona workshops, just south of Seattle. As a recent graduate of the Epona Apprenticeship program, I volunteered to help facilitate some of the group sessions during this class. Peggy, the host, had a herd of Tennessee Walking Horses and I was excited by the idea of getting to spend time with this gaited breed.

During the course of the workshop, I remember Peggy commenting that Grace was the lead mare, and in fact, *her* very first horse. I heard the horse handlers remark that Grace wouldn't let them catch her, that she didn't seem pleased about sharing time with humans. To be honest, I don't remember much of Grace, as I'd been captivated by her daughter Savannah.

Savannah was a stunning, dark black beauty who was more than happy to listen to the stories I would tell her about what my life would be like when I had horses of my own. She was my roommate so to speak, as her paddock was right beside the van I slept in. Even after I climbed into bed, I could whisper to her out the window and fall asleep to the sound of her movements as she grazed, breathed, and slept.

After the workshop, I made my way home, back up the I-5 through the border crossing in Sumas, Washington. The time at Peggy's made my empty pastures seem all the more barren, but I trusted that in time, the horses, my horses, would come. It had been just over a year since my husband Greg and I had moved our young family onto this land, a beautiful five acres in Maple Ridge, a little horse town 40 minutes east of Vancouver, BC, where there are still street signs asking motorists to watch for horses on our roads. My dream was to run my private practice from home. Horses had been my co-therapists and co-teachers for the last four years in other locations. Now, the need for horses at this home seemed obvious.

Getting Greg to build our first home in a Maple Ridge subdivision was a feat in itself. He had grown up in the city, and to him, Maple Ridge was WAAAAAAYYYY OUT THERRRRRRE. When it came time to have the "move to an acreage discussion," well that was a whole different ball game.

"The horses will pay for themselves," I told him.

"Mmmm hmmmm," he'd reply.

So after Seattle, I began the search for "my horse" in earnest. I poured through magazines, read articles, searched the net, and went to shows. I knew my horse was out there somewhere. I just had to *find* him or her.

About a year into my search, I brought home a magazine about the romantic breeds, the Friesians, Iberian Horses, and the Gypsy Vanners. Here they were, all in one issue, the horses that literally took my breath away as I imagined riding after a dragon on my feathered black mount. Inside was an article by Susan Elliott, a woman who lived in Minnesota, detailing her story of being found by her Friesian stallion, Gibraltar.

The dreamer in me was deeply moved. I emailed her right away. We began to connect about possibilities and Susan told me about Wisdom, her beautiful white mare. The more I learned about Wisdom the more compelled I felt to meet her, so Susan and I arranged for a visit. I was presenting at the Horses and Healing Conference in a couple of months so I could fly into St. Paul on my way home. "Wow," I thought. "It's happening."

After setting this date, I started to have dreams about Wisdom. I felt connected to her even though we hadn't met. I'd talk to Susan about the progress on our property. The shelter was being built, the fencing put in. It was becoming real.

In April, a month before my trip east, I got an email from Susan. Wisdom had died. They were unsure what had happened. Susan was wracked with grief. I felt numb. Then I felt betrayed. Not by Susan or Wisdom, but by whatever it was that called itself Divine. How could this happen? How could I wait for so long, all my life, for this dream to be realized, only to have it taken away? I grieved. I stumbled. An empty space formed in my heart.

It was with mixed feelings that I drove south past Seattle, just a few weeks later. Peggy's mare Ebby was supposed to foal that day, a miracle I hadn't witnessed since I was a child… but my heart carried an emptiness, and this impending life seemed to make the emptiness more real.

The farm was quiet when I arrived. There were horses grazing contentedly on the spring grass and I waved at them as I went in search of Peggy. I found her leaning over the fence, her head bent in wonder. "Come meet Dewey," she said, her face shining with delight.

I joined her at the fence and looked down into the stall. There, lying upon the fresh straw was a little chestnut angel, all eyelashes and legs. He looked up at me and I smiled. The empty space in my heart became less empty, as his cherubic face settled there.

After marveling at the joy of new life, Peggy and I went inside for a visit. I told her that my little piece of heaven was finally ready for horses, and then I told her about Wisdom. We sat quietly for a while before Peggy asked, "What are you going to do about horses?"

"I don't know. Why? Are you going to give me Savannah?" I mused, with a limp attempt at levity.

"No," she said. "But what about Grace?"

"Grace??? ... GRACE! ... But Grace doesn't even like people!" I exclaimed. I couldn't believe what Peggy was saying. Didn't she know my little herd would be working with all kinds of people? Kids with autism, cancer survivors, corporate teams... Didn't she know that my husband and young daughters knew nothing of horses, so our horses would have to be gentle and kind?

Didn't she know that my herd would need to be comprised of horses who loved humans? If I could only have two, there would be no room for a horse like Grace.

I mean, she certainly had to know Grace was not the Andalusian or the Friesian I'd been dreaming of.

GRACE!!! How could Grace fit into my plans, into my life?

My internal rant was interrupted by Peggy's invitation to go out to the herd. "Let's go and see her," she said.

I nodded, but wondered what was the point.

Peggy opened the gate to the pasture where most of the herd was grazing. The lead mare lifted her head, then walked toward us. She came closer and closer, intent-full and direct. She stopped right in front of me, laying her head upon my shoulder. I could feel my heart swell beyond the boundary of my chest.

Wide eyed, Peggy whispered that she'd never seen Grace do anything like this before. In turn, I whispered I had never felt anything like this before, yet as soon as I'd said those words, I knew they weren't true, for there was a familiarity that my heart remembered, something beyond the limits of my mind.

I looked down at her head and followed the line of her neck to her powerful coffee black body. We stood in silence for what was both a moment and a lifetime. And then my head took me out of my heart as an image of Grace tried to replace the dream images I'd held for so long.

The trip home passed in an instant. I mumbled something to the border guard as I crossed the 49th parallel. Turning into our driveway, I looked at the newly fenced pasture, empty with possibility. Was it really supposed to be Grace grazing there?

Peggy had invited me to think about Grace and think I did. I thought about all of the reasons why she didn't fit. If I could only have a couple of horses, why shouldn't I wait for the horse of my dreams? I felt like an indignant child being told what to do, but in spite of what I knew - far beneath my conscious mind - I was going to choose something else just to prove that I could. Not that anyone was telling me what to do, but there was a sense of something powerful at the edge of my awareness, and of it, I wanted no part.

On a conscious level, I did have an idea… something that could help me make my decision about Grace. I'd invite my sister Lisa to come with me to Peggy's. That way, I'd see if Grace could pass the "Lisa Test".

My sister was notorious for her easy going nature with animals. Even my old dog Kody, the kindest of labs and a therapist in his own right, had her number. We used to tease Lisa when she stayed over at our house because we'd arise late and afresh to find her sitting in the kitchen, bleary eyed and sleepy. Apparently, on every occasion, Kody would leave our room in the wee hours and go to where Lisa was sleeping. He'd softly place his head on the bed next to hers and breathe and sigh until she woke up. She'd stumble out of bed and take him for a walk, complaining to us when we got up that he just didn't seem to be able to make it through the night. Greg and I would chuckle because we were self-proclaimed night owls and Kody would sleep soundly with us until hours that are too late to mention.

Would Grace take advantage of Lisa's inexperience? We'd find out in a couple of weeks as Lisa and I had planned a trip to Seattle to see *Cavalia*, the incredible Cirque du Soleil show with horses. We could stop in at Peggy's and then head back for the show.

Lisa and I arrived at the farm around noon. I went to the house to find Peggy while Lisa watched young Dewey bounce around in his paddock. Peg wasn't in the house so we walked over to the barn. Grace was there, standing in a stall with her head out in the aisle. I heard a soft nicker as I approached.

"I knew you were coming," said Peggy, rounding the corner of the barn.

"Of course you knew we were coming," I teased. "We arranged this a week ago."

"No," she said. "I knew you were coming because Grace left the herd and was staring down the driveway for the last 30 minutes, so I brought her up here to get her brushed."

"Oh…" was all I could manage.

Peggy tacked up Grace and led her into the arena. She stood quietly while Lisa mounted. I watched Grace while Peggy coached Lisa in what to do. Grace's body moved powerfully yet tenderly as she carried Lisa around the arena. Peg had set up a line of orange cones and I watched as Grace wound in and out of them. The only aid Lisa offered was to look in the direction she wanted to go.

Lisa smiled as she dismounted. "That was fun," she said. Grace had passed the Lisa test.

"Do you want to ride her Sandra?" Peggy asked.

"No thank you. I don't need to," I replied.

Our time at the farm evaporated and we had to leave to get to the show. I thanked Peggy, and Grace, and said I'd *be in touch*. As I write this now, I realize that was the key. I'd been so in my head about this decision that what I'd truly been was OUT OF TOUCH. Out of touch with what my heart and body knew: that I belonged to this mare. She was the horse of my dreams. All I had to do was remember… remember there was a power greater than myself directing this. For it was not about me choosing a horse. It was about allowing myself to be found by one, to be chosen. This idea frightened me a little at first, and then I felt taken over by it.

I'm not sure how much time passed, but Peg and I made arrangements for Grace to be trailered north. I sat by the front window, listening and watching for the hauler to arrive. Greg would pass in and out of the room, doing a little watching of his own.

Finally, I heard it. An unfamiliar grumble as the truck and trailer groaned up our hill. As I saw the white truck pull into view, I shouted, "SHE'S HERE!" I leapt off the couch and reached for my shoes. Tears streamed down my face.

"WOW. You're really excited about this," Greg said.

"This is my dream come true," I cried.

"I thought I was your dream come true," he teased.

And as I ran out the door I called back with a smile, "I've been dreaming of horses long before I dreamed of you!"

My heart remembered a little more...

It was magic. There was a horse on my lawn. Her dark chocolate body was framed by a background of green. She seemed so at peace. She'd blow and sigh as she searched for the tastiest blades. My daughters, seven and five at the time, flitted around her like dancing butterflies. Grace would take them in with her deep knowing eyes and then return her head to the earth.

My life had changed. I had changed. I could feel myself opening. I remembered a bit more.

That first night, after Grace arrived, I climbed into bed with all of her papers. I wanted to read every word before I fell asleep, although I was so excited, I didn't know if sleep would find me.

I read vet reports and details of where she was born. Then I opened her registration papers. Beside "Name" was typed: *A Grace Remembered.*

There it was, in black and white; the title of our story. At that point I had no idea about the countless chapters Grace would help me write, metaphorically, until now. I was also unaware of the many ways she would help others, empowering them to step forward with purpose, strength... and grace.

Carolyn Myss, on her *Channeling Grace* CD series describes grace as being the breath of God, "... an invisible essence beyond intellect that moves swiftly amongst us... Grace is real and tangible. It's ready to dramatically transform your life at any time – if you are willing to acknowledge it."

Now granted, she's not talking about the horse I share my life with, but in my mind and heart, her grace and my Grace are one and the same. When I was ready to acknowledge her, my life was dramatically transformed. Not in a way that someone who viewed me from a distance would recognize, and initially not in a way that I recognized for myself, but with time and Grace's tutelage, I've learned that great change does not have to come in the aftermath of a storm, it can occur within the softness of a snowflake or in the mirror of a horse's eye, when we first see ourselves reflected there. And reflected there, I was.

One of the activities I share, when I'm teaching students how to connect with their horses, or perhaps with their inner horse, involves taking dictation. During one particular class, the woman who thought she was to work with Grace heard very distinctly that she was to go and work with the dog. In no way was this a slight. Guinness, our English Mastiff, was a prophet in his own right. This left Grace without a partner, to wander loose around the lawn. In short time she was beside me, nudging my binder with her nose. Everyone else was engrossed in their writing. Maybe I could take a little dictation myself. I opened to a clean page, a tabula rasa. Words flowed from my pen without thought...

Grace to Sandra

Winter will be coming soon.
Come into my womb.
I will carry you until you are ready for rebirth.
It is painful, the leaving of one world for another.
You breathe in the liquid air, then gasp awake the mountains.
The eagle knows you, and the butterfly...
Now, plant your seeds in my earth.

When it was my turn to read the prose aloud, I did in fact gasp. Writing it was one thing, reading it another. And now that the words had been spoken, I felt unsettled by their meaning. I looked over at Grace. My heart remembered... I'd been chosen. Chosen not only by this beautiful mare, but by life itself. A veil lifted and I saw my history anew. I recognized that life had reclaimed me over and again, even though there'd been times when I'd felt thrown away. Each reclamation was in fact a rebirth, a leaving of one world for another. Recognizing this, I felt humbled. Gratitude filled my heart.

Grace continued to share her wisdom with me and often it came through the experiences she offered others. Although I was becoming familiar with her amazing repertoire, people who were meeting her for the first time were often unprepared.

A friend of mine called me, asking to come out for a visit. He had just been diagnosed with cancer, and although he had never spent time with horses, he felt he needed to today.

When Yves arrived, we walked out to the field where two horses were grazing. Our family had grown by one when Chiron arrived just weeks after Grace, and in atypical fashion, he kept his head down and ate as Grace walked directly toward us. Having been on the receiving end of her walk, I knew what to expect, but Yves grabbed my arm and asked if he was safe. I assured him that he was as Grace stopped right in front of him. Putting her nose to his chest, Grace breathed warm breath at his heart. Yves' grip loosened slightly. She then dropped her head to the area beneath his belt. Yves froze, except for his fingers, which dug into my arms.

"It's okay," I whispered. His grip loosened slightly.

We must have stood there for fifteen minutes, unmoving except to breathe. Although Yves still held my arm, he began to relax. Eventually he closed his eyes. Grace breathed deep, warm breaths. She exhaled with force and intention.

"She knows," he sighed.

"I have no doubt," I sighed back.

Yves smiled.

Moments later, Grace dropped her head to his feet and then walked away. Yves and I held each other. There were no words. Afterward, Yves climbed into his car and drove away, down the hill, his car disappearing behind Grace's body. She lifted her head and watched with me.

This time *our* hearts remembered.

As a school counselor, I have the opportunity to be in and out of many classrooms and therefore I get to know and meet many children and many teachers. One day while I was out on supervision, I heard screaming. I looked around as Matthew burst forth from behind the school. He was on the run and right behind him followed his ever loving support teacher. He smiled as she wrapped her arms around him and they carried on toward the playground. Matthew had autism and running off at random was a concern for all of us. It was hoped that if he could develop more of a relationship with the people and places in his life, he would run away less, and respond to people more. We talked with his family about animal therapy and they thought bringing him out to meet the horses would be a wonderful idea.

When Matthew arrived, he was vocalizing loudly. Guinness went to greet him and Matthew was mesmerized for a moment by his drool. Ever patient and kind, Guinness allowed the poking fingers to grab at his mouth. The bunnies, however, weren't as understanding about their ears.

When it came time to introduce Matthew to the horses, he was unaffected by their size and, except for the brief drool moment, the screaming had yet to stop. I wondered silently if there would be anything here for him and, mid-thought, Grace walked up to him and put her nose to his head. Quiet. Like a switch had been turned. Matthew kept his head bowed while Grace whiffled his hair. Quiet.

We lifted Matthew into the saddle. Side walkers took their positions and we walked across the lawn. The only sound we could hear was Grace's footfall on the grass. As we carried on with our walkabout, I started to hear a hum. I looked around to see where the sound was coming from and caught the eyes of one of the support teachers. We both looked up. The sound was coming from Matthew. He was humming. Not the kind of humming that accompanies disassociation, but the kind of humming that comes from a place of utter joy.

There he was, sitting atop this rolling sea – for when Grace moves out it is like riding an ocean swell – with a smile on his face and a song in his heart. When we stopped he put his hand on her neck. Quiet. Smiles.

His heart remembered.

The qualities I saw in Grace during that first Epona workshop, the ones that made me think she could never fit, I now see and know as her gifts. She models healthy boundaries like no-one I know. Saying no is an art form for Grace and she insists on each of us standing in our power. But she'll hold us tenderly when we need to grieve and love us when we need to be loved. She is an invisible essence who takes us beyond intellect, and a tangible force who walks beside us, inspiring hope and catalyzing joy.

Grace has changed the way I look at things and in turn the things I look at have changed. Instead of focusing on what is not, I focus on what is, and what can be. I've learned that by shifting my perspectives, I can see, and feel, so much more.

A Grace Remembered… she sees the grace in all things and inspires me to do the same.

Grace, Remembered

With a heart full of gratitude to my incredible family. I love you. And to Grace... Thank you for taking me under your tutelage... and for helping my heart remember.

About
Sandra Wallin

Sandra Wallin has been learning from horses, in one way or another, her entire life, but it wasn't until Grace and Chiron arrived that her apprenticeship truly began. Sandra claims Grace has taught her to be a better person and Chiron is teaching her to be a better horse, and as she learns, so she teaches, in her Equine Guided Development programs at Chiron's Way.

Chiron's Way is located on a little piece of heaven some 40 minutes east of Vancouver, BC. Here you'll find programs that empower perspectives and accelerate personal and team growth. Sandra often hears from her urban clients how much they appreciate the outdoor classroom, that simply being on the land enables them to feel more connected to themselves, each other, and their learning. As a lifelong learner herself, Sandra has had the privilege of studying with many leaders in the field of Equine Guided Learning and Wellness. She is an Epona Approved Instructor and has Bachelor's degrees in Science and Education, and a Master's Degree in Counseling Psychology.

Sandra is a Registered Clinical Counselor, an educator, and a presenter, who divides her professional time between a private practice, working as an educator/counselor in a local school district, and teaching Equine Guided Development and PSYCH-K, locally and internationally. Her clients range from middle school students to corporate executives and she currently sits on a Canadian Therapeutic Riding Association (CanTRA) committee helping to develop guidelines for the ethical practice of Equine Facilitated Wellness in Canada.

Sandra is a certified PSYCH-K Instructor, one of forty worldwide. She became passionate about PSYCH-K after a riding accident in May of 2008 left her unconscious and broken. Unable to get out to her horses, she began to use, with herself, the processes she had been sharing with her clients. Her healing progressed exponentially. As a result, Sandra now integrates PSYCH-K with her equine practice, teaching students how to use their subconscious to become more horse conscious, and in turn, create and live the lives they've imagined, with their horses and beyond.

To learn more about Chiron's Way programs, or to sponsor a class in your community, please contact Sandra at chironsway@shaw.ca or visit www.chironsway.com.

Opposites Attract

By Debra A. Saum

If there's one thing I've discovered by observing hundreds of animal/ human relationships, it's this: opposites really do attract. Take my horse Romeo for example. When we first met, our relationship read something like this: "Gorgeous, big, lame, grumpy retired show horse who is skeptical of humans, meets altruistic, Animal Intuitive/green horse owner who wants to help him find true partnership."

I'll always remember the day we met. Following a hunch that he might be the horse who'd been coming to me in my dreams, I responded to his For Sale ad. Standing there in all his 16+ hands of handsome equine masculinity, I was struck with how emotionally unavailable he was. "Boy, he's big," I thought. "That's a whole lot of not wanting to get to know me standing there."

Then I rode him. And there it was. That feeling. Like we'd been doing this our entire lives.

Little did I realize what I was getting us into.

From the beginning, Romeo and I were challenged with not only the arthritis that his show career had bequeathed him, but the rigid pessimism he'd developed during his many years of service. I knew he secretly carried a desire to connect with someone special, but I also knew it would take everything I had as an Animal Intuitive to help him unlock that strong hold he had on his heart.

I was 56 years old, just returning to my enchantment with horses. During my childhood in the 1960's my dad moved us to the sticks of East County in San Diego, California and bought us a horse, hoping that my infatuation with all things equine would supersede my teenage lust for boys. It worked. I fell in love with our sweet Misty, a Quarter Horse-Morgan cross who was willing to do all the crazy, dangerous things a young girl with no horse sense could think of. I knew absolutely nothing about horses when

Misty came into my life, and sadly, didn't know much more when she left it just a short time later. My dad died at the far-too-early age of 36. I was only 16; the oldest of three kids, and my grieving mother was completely overwhelmed with the loss of her beloved husband. Misty found a new home and my dreams of becoming Annie Oakley ended there.

Fast forward 40 years. A series of clairvoyant dreams involving a horse who kept searching for me, along with a fortuitous visit from my young nieces catapulted me right back to the magical world of horses. Little did I know that by scheduling riding lessons for them, it would be me who'd fall head over heals for the equine spirit.

Ending up looking for my own horse on *dreamhorse.com* a year later was no coincidence. There he was: First Class Romeo, a 14 year-old, beautiful, big, chestnut Quarter Horse.

And lame as they come.

"Don't buy this horse," was the vet's final prognosis after Romeo's pre-purchase exam. So I did what every intelligent, inexperienced horsewoman would do. I bought him. And as it turned out, our journey became nothing short of miraculous. Not only in spite of, but perhaps because of our differences, Romeo and I found a kind of unity that only comes when two individuals surrender to something greater than themselves.

I am an effusively affectionate person. A hugger, a shoulder toucher, and a hand grasper, my first urge when meeting someone, be it horse, dog, person, or cat is to reach out and touch them. My hands are such important tools in my work. The feel of the paint brush as I create an animal portrait, the caress of someone's companion as I conduct an Animal Communication session; I rely on my sense of touch to transmit telepathic information. I can't imagine trying to navigate the sometimes complicated world of psychic conversation without using my hands.

Fortunately for me and my daily quota of hugs and kisses, all the animals in my life, including those who belong to friends, neighbors, clients, etc., appreciate my adoration of them. At home I have raised all my fur children to love and adore being loved and adored. Daily love fests are not only common in our home, they're a mutual celebration.

When meeting an animal for the first time however, I am respectful of their need for autonomy. The same invisible bubble most humans carry around them to define their personal space also surrounds animals. When greeting an animal I've never met, I respect their boundaries, giving them time to check me out. Without fail, they eventually want to be stroked or lovingly petted once they get to know me.

I usually start out with a sincere greeting. "Hello! You are such a handsome dog! I bet you get compliments all the time!"

"Hello big guy! Aren't you just the sweetest horse I've ever met! Such a soft eye."

"Hi there kitter. What a beautiful coat you have! You must love to be brushed."

Animals need positive strokes just like us humans. I've never met an animal who didn't respond to a genuine display of positive attention.

Except for Romeo.

It was painfully obvious that his idea of emotional expression from the humans in his life was based on being disciplined or corrected.

Hand swats.

Spur jabs.

Smacks with the reigns.

Barking orders.

Western horsemanship training can mean stern and sometimes rough handling for the horse. That's not to say Romeo's previous human family didn't appreciate him, but they were influenced by old-line attitudes. Being overly affectionate wasn't normal. You didn't tell your horse you loved him. You told him to walk, trot, lope, and whoa. As a result, Romeo's opinion of human touch could be summed up in one word: irritating.

Thankfully I was over the moon for my horse. So from the time Romeo and I began our journey together, I respected his need for emotional aloofness and loved him anyway. Being the Queen of Touch however, it was an enormous challenge.

One day, not long after I purchased Romeo, I was grooming him. He was sullenly quiet, retreated into his own world, when suddenly that handsome head of his whipped around and snapped hard at the air around my hands. It was an obvious and direct communication, albeit confusing and troubling.

I was taken aback. Literally. I stepped back and just looked at him.

It wasn't the first time a horse had tried to bite me, but it was Romeo's reaction to his own assault that startled me so. In one lightning jerk, he whipped his head away from the offensive air-nip. The look in his bulging eyes as he waited for me to smack him said it all: "Here it comes. Hit me."

I stood there for a moment, dumbfounded and heartbroken. How many hundreds of times had he been hit in the head or neck for trying to communicate?

Don't get me wrong. Horses who bite are dangerous and there are a host of prescribed disciplinary actions recommended for dealing with it. For every horse that has ever tried to bite someone, there are at least twice as many ways to handle it. But not all methods are suited for all horses.

So what to do about this bad habit? I tried several different approaches with Romeo. He would try to nip. I would respond with a firm, but loving voice: "No bites, Romeo."

Stroke, stroke. Pat, pat. Brush, brush, all the while telling him not to bite me, sending him silent, but firm telepathic tones of disapproval, letting him know I wouldn't hit him for it. I was, after all, the one who loved him. I was special. I was the horse whisperer he'd always needed and we'd just telepathically psych this thing out.

It worked for about a milla-second.

As a horse who (a) didn't like to be touched and (b) was dominant and (c) pessimistic about humans, this approach made *him* more cranky and *me* more confused.

Next, I tried the "I'm going to ignore your attempt to engage me in a reaction to that nip" approach. It worked for a while. At least he stopped with his alarming, backward head jerk, since he realized the anticipated whack wasn't coming.

But it was only a matter of time before he started again with not only air-nips, but full contact nips; well placed pinches that left little marks on my skin. And they weren't saved only for grooming time or for just me. He'd do it from his stall. People would walk by and he'd pin his ears, showing his teeth. He became known as the horse that might bite, so stay clear.

When a horse is aggressively mouthy with humans, it's a sure sign there's trouble in paradise. It can mean teeth problems, pain or discomfort, extreme unhappiness with his or her environment, or a bad habit learned when they were young.

Or all of the above.

There are many horse owners who don't take the time to understand even one of the reasons why this blatant form of communication is coming from their horse.

I'm not one of them.

After experimenting with a variety of approaches, only to have Romeo's pretend nips and bites escalate, I began to look at it from a different perspective: his.

Romeo is a mouthy horse. He's also a very smart horse with an active mind and a strong personality. He uses those lips of his and that soft muzzle to communicate his wants and needs and it's up to me to interpret what he's saying.

Nibble, nibble. Doodle, doodle. Chew, Chew.

When we are walking in-hand or standing around and that big ole' mouth of his gets going, he's usually telling me it's time to do something different, or it's time to go say hello to one of the other horses, or it's time for lunch or he has to pee, or I'm not paying attention, or he's not paying attention, or… the list goes on. His mouth is also how he tells me about his pain levels from day to day. When he's sore from his arthritis, he wants to chew on the brushes, his lead rope, the reins, anything within reach. I've learned that by listening to him, and I mean really absorbing what he's telling me with that mouth, he doesn't have to resort to nips or bites or chewing.

As I've explained to so many other horse owners whose equine companions are also mouthy, telepathic communication combined with empathic understanding is essential in comprehending your horse's sometimes irritating and garrulous conduct. That mouthy behavior *always* means something. It's one of their most effective communication tools. Listen up, tune in, and you just might be surprised by what your horse is trying to tell you each time that mouth of his or hers gets going.

Over time, Romeo and I developed a promise we could both respect. It goes like this: I agree to listen to his overactive mouth and he agrees to not get pushy with it. There are days we also agree to disagree and I may have to remind him with "the look", but we no longer participate in the exhausting Battle of the Nip.

Understanding Romeo's mouthy habits was one thing. Overcoming our differences about affection was another story altogether. He was not a horse who looked forward to the praise and tenderness I so desperately wanted to shower upon him. His idea of adulation was a pat.

One. Not two and never three or more.

Even the words "Good Boy" would bug him. And because I am the affectionate, compliment-giving, overly exuberant cheerleader that I am, praise is my middle name. I'd tell him he was a good boy whenever he even looked like he was thinking about being cooperative.

"You are such a good boy, Rome's. I'm so proud of you."

He'd hear those verbal praises and tighten up. That boy could give the arctic version of a cold shoulder that would freeze anybody out.

"Don't you tell me I'm a good boy. You don't mean it."

Well stubbornness goes both ways. With Romeo's every dismissal of my compliments I dug in my heels and gave him more. It was a test of wills. He'd met his match. I teasingly told him if he'd never heard the phrase "kill them with kindness" he was about to become the victim of affection abuse. Tortured by too much love, he'd expire from excessive adoration.

For months I respected his need for space, but also honored my own need for closeness. One of the ways I showed him this was a "free-love" ritual I made up just for him. A throw back to my hippie days of early adulthood, I'd approach him after our grooming sessions with slow, gentle strokes along his beautiful neck, followed by a full body hug in which I'd gently step into his massive chest, tenderly press myself against him, wrapping my arms around his mane. I called them our "heart to heart" hugs.

"My heart touching your heart, boy," I'd tell him.

I'd also soften him up during his grooming. I'd use what I cheerfully called his "softie brushes", giving him a full body massage to rub away all the grumpiness. Whispering sweet nothings in his ears, I reminded him he was special, handsome, and how every time I saw him, he took my breath away. Which was actually the truth. I couldn't help it; almost every time I'd look at him, my breath would catch. I knew he must notice it and whether or not he acknowledged it, I was convinced my obvious infatuation with him was having positive effects on that closed up heart of his.

There was also my verbal communication. Daily, I was mindful about how I spoke to him, the tone of my voice conveying genuine love and commitment to him. Every time I greeted him, I'd call out affectionately, "Hey Rome's! How's my boy? Whatcha doin' darlin'? Are you gonna come say hi?"

The lilting quality of my voice spoke sincere devotion. And I didn't give up on the "good boy" praises, no matter how minuscule an effort he gave me.

I also began using treats with him. Going completely against everything he'd ever been taught before me, I wasn't sure how it would work.

"Back up boy."

As a winner of ribbons in Showmanship Class this was old hat. He'd done it a million times.

"Good Boy!!"

I exclaimed my delight and surprise as though it was the first time he'd ever done this incredulous task. I immediately offered a horse cookie in my outstretched palm. He took one surprised look at it and with one loud crunch downed that sucker. We repeated this exercise a few more times until I could tell he believed he wasn't hallucinating.

"Yup, you're gonna start getting treats for when it works between us boy. You deserve it."

Probably the most important thing I did to help Romeo loosen up his heart and accept human kindness was to practice telepathy. Horses are the masters of psychic transmission; their entire world is influenced by the sixth sense. And I am, for Pete's sake, an Animal Intuitive. How hard could this be?

"You're not going to *talk* to me today are you?"

This was his greeting on more than one occasion. The irony, of course, being that we were using telepathic communication to talk about not talking. So I just waited him out. I promised to respect his need for psychic space just as I respected his intense desire for physical distance. I avoided telepathic conversations that required him to engage with me, but I continued using psychic communication as a way of establishing a deeper bond between us.

During our hours together when we'd take hand-walks, practice fun games at liberty, or enjoy the occasional ride in the arena where the soft footing was easy on his arthritic joints, I'd send him a constant stream of telepathic sweetness, bathing him with thoughts of love, forgiveness, and gratitude. When I was home at night, I'd do a meditation before going to sleep, sending him visions of golden light, imagining a vibrating cord of goodness traveling from my heart to his like a lifeline. I still practice this meditation even today. It is a delicious way to end the day and has proven to be one of the most powerful tools for not only Romeo's development, but my own.

And then there were the paintings. Romeo is a stunning horse. His beautiful long neck, shining coat, muscular body, and inquisitive eye make him the perfect model for equine portraits. I created several paintings of him, not only as examples of horse art for my portfolio and website, but for the healing that I knew they would induce in our relationship. All art has the power to profoundly affect people. I've learned over the years that my art stimulates telepathic, empathic, and spiritual communication between the animal in the painting and the humans who gaze upon the canvas. The numerous psychic conversations between me and the animal while I am painting them carry a frequency that lives on in the canvas, stimulating further psycho-sensory communication.

I knew that by creating beautiful artwork of my most cherished boy and displaying those portraits throughout my studio and home, Romeo and I could connect on profoundly deep levels. To this day, every time I look at one of his portraits I think about how much he means to me. His portraits are a psychic telephone line allowing thoughts of love and appreciation to flow between us.

Debra A. Saum, Romeo

The change in Romeo's attitudes about experiencing real love from his human partner was subtle and slow. It was more the absence of crankiness I first began to notice. He wasn't really returning my affections as much as he wasn't giving me the stink eye all the time. It was almost a year later when something happened that will live in my heart forever.

Every day when I arrive at the barn and after my effervescent, verbal greeting to him as I am walking toward his paddock, I open his gate and step into his corral. I stand comfortably and patiently, waiting for him to come up and say hello. He knows I have cookies or carrots in my pockets, so some days the coming up to say hello is really, "Got treats?"

Fine by me. There are also days he's just glad to see me.

We walk around, me exploring his corral for signs of good poops, checking on his water and the shavings in his stall. He follows me around, sometimes curious, sometimes just wanting to hang out, sometimes thinking a carrot is calling him. We finish by lounging around, enjoying each other's company before we go into the round pen, arena, or out for a walk.

This day we were standing together, soaking up the sun. He was to my right; I was at his head. It was a delicate, peaceful moment. I was completely absorbed in the feelings of sunshine on my face, caught up in our quiet reverie.

I felt a soft, tiny, and ever so gentle tug on my shirt.

I looked down.

It was Romeo.

He had very carefully gathered up a tiny bit of material from the front of my garment in his teeth and was simply, but mindfully hanging on.

No tug.

No nip.

No where-are-the-cookies.

No let's-do-something-else.

Just hanging on… wanting to get closer… needing to connect.

"I love you too, boy," I said with a catch in my throat. I stroked him and turned my cheek to rest on his neck, giving him soft smooches all around his eye and head. He stood stone still, soaking it up. The look on his face told me how deeply he was enjoying this mutual display of affection. I quietly lifted my face, turned it back toward the sun, and we stood in peaceful union like that, him continuing to clutch my shirt. You could feel the love pulsing between us, surrounding us like a Hollywood moment.

It's then I realized something about affection and how opposites attract.

Not every person or animal shows his or her appreciation in the same way. For the millions of individuals who express their feelings, there are a million different ways to do it.

You say tomato and I say tomauto.

I happen to fall into the over-the-top category of affection. My amorous demonstrations of enthusiasm are a reflection of my zest for life and my sincere need to share it with others. Romeo on the other hand, is in the category of chivalrous and contained. I recognized in that moment that my past assumptions about the differences between Romeo and I being an obstacle to us sharing affection had been a mistake. After all, here we were, standing side-by-side, sharing love and friendship. Mutual admiration and gratitude was the powerful, binding moment.

It had been there all along. I had only to look within my own heart to see the opening of his.

From that day on, Romeo and I grew increasingly bonded, our partnership richly brimming with affection, and his desire for attention blossoming. One day several months later, I decided to take it up a notch. I came up with a brilliant, albeit unconventional idea of teaching him how to show affection on cue. Romeo is an outrageously curious horse with a wonderfully quick mind who relishes in learning new things instantly. One of the things I love most about him is his desire to excel with new tasks, and I was confident we could design a fun game that allowed us both to express our growing affection for each other.

We called it "Gimme Kiss". It was not the most effective training technique for winning copious awards in the Show Ring, but was a private and deliciously decadent practice between horse and human.

The idea came to me one day while standing outside Romeo's paddock Dutch door. Each day before I say goodbye to him we stand there for a moment, looking out at the hillside across from his corral, just marinating in the mellow sweetness of our hours spent together that day. He hangs his head over the top of the door and I stand to his left, both of us facing out. I send him telepathic messages of love and thankfulness and he waits for the pat on his cheek, the stroke on his neck, and the "see you tomorrow boy" he knows will come right before I leave for home.

The thought hit me. "I wonder if I could teach him to give me a kiss?"

I'd been giving him daily smooches on the side of his muzzle ever since our magical moment in the sun when he stood clutching my shirt. I'd place my kisses on that delicate soft spot right above the corner of his lip along the curve of his nose. Breathing in his enchanting scent, I'd gently touch my lips in an intimate whisper of appreciation and love. We'd indulge in this little love fest following a good ride or sometimes during grooming. He loves it.

"What if I could ask him to give me his muzzle on cue, so he can have his kiss?"

I asked him to step closer and to exchange his breath with me, leaning my face close to him while giving him visual pictures of what I wanted. He pulled away, wondering what to do. This was something altogether new. We'd exchanged breath many times before, but always by his direction. This time, it was me doing the directing. I asked again, now with a waiting carrot.

"Gimme a kiss, boy. I've got a carrot for you if you'll give me your nose."

He curiously leaned toward my head, placing his nostrils next to mine. We exchanged breath for just a second and then he slowly pulled away again, looking at me quizzically.

"Good boy!"

I gave him the piece of carrot and asked him again. He didn't hesitate. I quickly landed a gentle kiss on his muzzle and awarded him with another carrot. He stepped closer, stretching his beautiful, long neck, pressing those chops against my cheek. His ears were perked forward, his eyes dancing with sheer delight as he looked down at me, realizing what I wanted.

I looked directly into those eyes as I inched my face up toward his, giving him light smooches all along his cheek and making squeaky kissing noises as I planted them on his soft skin. His expression came alive with pure bliss, the enjoyment of this delightful new game palpable. I was struck by how much joy his whole body was exuding. I'd only seen this kind of delectable satisfaction in him a few other times, like after we'd conquered a particularly complicated pattern during our liberty work, or after a nice long bath (one of his favorite activities) in which we'd goofed off in the water, both ending up soaked and content.

I knew that exuberant look in his eyes. It meant he was beaming with accomplishment, completely enchanted by the moment of togetherness and unity we had just created. I felt it too. That unmistakable feeling of knowing you and your horse just did something utterly in unison. It didn't matter that it was something as simple as sharing affection, or something as silly as Gimme Kiss.

That moment represented the ultimate connection between horse and human… the realization of love and partnership that only comes when the heart and soul of two individuals blend as one. It's the dream we all have as horse lovers; the moment of harmony and union we all strive for in the relationships with our beloved equine companions.

Little did I know when Romeo first came into my life, two opposites thrown together in a divinely orchestrated affiliation, that it would be our noticeable differences that would end up pulling us together. As our acceptance of each other reached beyond all bounds, our opposing attributes finally became our ultimate strengths. Romeo taught me how to enjoy a new kind of quiet affection for my horse, while I helped him find expression for the innermost feelings of his heart.

And true to the powerful way of the horse, it was the equine path of least resistance that ultimately helped us to become two souls united in unconditional love. During the many silent moments in which we learned to embrace being genuinely present with each other, allowing our minds and hearts to recognize the peace of acceptance, we found a magical kinship that will sustain us forever.

To this day, Romeo loves to do the Gimme Kiss, especially with other people. The ultimate offering of trust, it melts my heart every time I reassure them it's just his way of showing affection.

I would like to thank my wonderful husband Bill Bargfrede. Our marriage is a true union of souls and a blessing of beauty and support. I am also infinitely grateful to Romeo for his depth of spirit, his magnificent resilience, and his genuine willingness to trust.

About
Debra A. Saum

Debra A. Saum is an internationally respected Animal Artist and Animal Intuitive whose award winning "Talking Art" is known for its revolutionary ability to ignite inter-species communication between the subjects in her portraits and the people who enjoy their vibrantly colorful canvases. Because of the telepathic conversations she has with the animals she paints, each portrait contains a frequency that stimulates further psycho sensory communication.

Her fascinating work affords her plenty of provocative and

Gimmee Kiss with Romeo

other-worldly moments. Like the time she conversed with a lion who sat no more than one foot away, talking about his heart-rendering message to mankind while she snapped the photographs she would later use to create his beautiful portrait. Or the conversations she had while painting Lassie, a spunky, deceased mare whose insightful messages from spirit talked about her charmed life in a well known Animal Sanctuary in upstate New York. Lassie's portrait hangs today in the Great Hall at Spring Farm Cares Sanctuary where she continues to conduct telepathic sessions with the students who go there to learn about Animal Communication. Or the moment when Alana, a beautiful Arabian filly, announced she was "smelling the emotions" when asked why horses like to investigate the manure of their herd members. Alana's matter of fact sixth-sense observations confirmed the higher consciousness that all animals possess.

Having painted hundreds of famous animals, horses, endangered wildlife, and the beloved pets of caring humans, Debra's 30+ years of experience has taught her that inter-species communication changes the way people think about not only the animals in their life, but about themselves and their relationship to the universe. In her popular Equine Communication Clinics and Animal Intuition Workshops, participants learn that telepathic interaction is a natural and powerful way to connect with all life. During her numerous television and radio appearances, viewers and listeners enjoy the sometimes humorous, but always poignant messages their favorite animals have for them. Upon completion of her "Talking Art" commissioned pieces, the lively conversations that transpired during the portraits' creation surprise and delight the humans who seek to better understand their four-legged companions.

Debra's introduction to horses was a unique adventure that started when she was a teenager, but was fortuitously interrupted, destined to return when she was a woman in her late 50's. Her serendipitous relationship with Romeo was her first real emersion into the world of horse ownership, and also the beginning of a personal transformation she could never have predicted. Inspired by how profoundly the equine spirit has touched her life, she has written a book about Romeo and the many enlightened animals she has encountered in her work. Titled *Trained by a Horse... A True Story about a Telepathic Gelding Named Romeo*, it will be available in 2010.

Debra resides in Encinitas, California with her husband and their three shelter kitties, Kilauea, Oscar, and Felix and their rescued lab, Sophie. Romeo lives at a facility nearby and continues to be her straight-shooting muse and confidante.

To contact Debra, visit www.debrasaum.com.

Alakaset or The Language of the Body

By Birgit Weskamp

On a late summer day on the California coast, after the fog had burned off and the air was fresh and warm, the trees still green but covered in dust, I found myself going uphill gingerly on the back of a horse. He walked, then trotted. The ride was not very comfortable, but he felt solid and soft and good under me. I was terrified at first at the lack of control that I seemed to have over his body and my own, but then got caught up in the thrill of the speed. We went faster and faster on this first trail ride. For some reason I trusted him, even though I had only just met him. As I felt us moving faster, I was filled with exhilaration. This is what I had been searching for, and it felt like I had found it, something new and exciting in my life to mark the entry into my fifties.

The prospect of turning fifty had filled me with anticipation. I did not worry too much about getting older, but wanted to pick a new hobby that was both enjoyable and challenging. Living on the Northern California Coast, I had briefly thought about kite surfing or maybe even paragliding, but for some reason horses kept coming to my mind.

My interest in riding had started with an email sent off to a trainer asking if she would offer lessons. She responded with an offer to meet at the Five Mile Coffee House on Freedom Boulevard in Corralitos. We met, shared a coffee, and I followed her out to the ranch. As we left, she said, "Don't worry if it takes a while to get there…"

I followed her along winding country roads, along apple orchards, storage barns, small farm houses, fields with cows and horses, then a dirt road, ever narrowing and very bumpy, under the canopy of oak trees, light filtering through the leaves creating shadow patterns on the road as it continued to wind narrower and narrower, along quince trees and willows and more apple orchards, a dry riverbed, and through an unlocked gate and up the hill where we stopped near a dilapidated farm house and an old horse trailer with two horses tied to it. One was smaller, brown, with black hair, some white on his feet and head, big brown eyes, stamping his foot, wanting to move; the other more solid, brown too, big belly, and more relaxed.

"Here is your horse, Alakaset. We call him Ala. And this is his companion, Gal. Let me tell you a little about how these horses work before we ride." And she told me some things, and more, and I listened, and then more to listen to, and then I got lost, there was so much to hear. I was overwhelmed and could not take in any more. At last, she said, "Let's go riding!"

Full of anticipation and not just a little terrified, I got on the smaller one of the brown horses and he felt surprisingly comfortable. I knew so little about these creatures that I could only access what was going on through what I felt – exhilaration to be moving, propelled forward by someone other than myself. My new teacher ponied me from her horse going up the hill, slow at first, me unsure, not always well balanced, humped forward protectively as we gathered speed, then with a big smile on my face as we sped up the hill.

We reached the top of the hill and entered a flat area overlooking Monterey Bay with Ford Ord and the Toro County Park hills in the background, then the gentle curve of the ocean on our right, framed by farmland with small buildings, redwoods, and oaks sprinkled across the panorama. I could feel the excitement spread through my body that I was viewing this sight from the back of a horse. We turned back and at the bottom of the hill, got off and walked the horses to the trailer to take off their saddles. My teacher let loose her horse, whereas my mount was taken to an enclosure.

"Why?" I asked.

"Well, he is a stallion, so he is best kept in his paddock while any of the mares are in heat."

"Where are the other horses?"

"Oh, they are somewhere on the property."

"You mean in their paddock?"

"No, they are not fenced in, they move over the 200 acres as the mood takes them."

"But don't they run away?"

"Not often. The food keeps them here and the neighbors are very understanding! And by the way, it is pretty extraordinary to ride a stallion on your first ride. But he is a very special horse."

I realized that I had come across a very unusual situation: loose horses living together in a herd, a stallion in their midst and used as a lesson horse for beginners – this really sounded like the adventure I had been looking for. I felt deeply drawn to this horse who had looked after me so well on my first ride, and felt the need to look after him too, right from the start, when I knew nothing of his history.

Experiencing this first ride already gave me a hint of how this "hobby" would influence my life. Not knowing anything about horses, I had to rely on my feelings – how my body felt on his back – and this ride brought to me the beginning of an awareness of my own body as a communication tool that had not always been there in my past as a university teacher and eventually a business person. As I learned more from Ala, I acquired a whole new nonverbal vocabulary: how to read his expressions, i.e. ears flicked back, tense nostrils, swiveling ears, tense back, engaged hind quarters, slight hesitation to put down his left front leg, sighing, licking, chewing, glazed over eyes, kind eyes. It all meant something, and if I did not understand it at that point, it did not follow that the horse's expression was without meaning, but rather that I had not yet learned his language.

From Ala, I more clearly learned the language of the body, which helped me read what went on with the humans around me, whether it was seeing the signs of concern in the wrinkle between the eyebrows of an employee before even a word was uttered, or the forced bright laughter of another employee masking an underlying issue. My interactions with Ala made me more aware of what was going on with others at a deeper level. As I tried to read this level just as information without judgment or defensiveness, it helped diffuse potentially difficult situations. I learned to accept my own discomfort in a situation simply as significant information about the status of that interaction.

I watched and learned, I rode and learned, I listened and learned, and it calmed me down after a crazy day at the office. My mind quieted when I turned the corner, saw the old farm house, the trailer, the stallion in his paddock, and the loose horses on their daily journey from one meadow to another, under oak and manzanita trees, with the farmland down below and the redwoods of the foothills behind us. The space crept into my body and calmed every cell, and I could just be, as the horses stood and watched and grazed. Nothing was asked of them, they just existed, eyes half closed, nose twitching with the flies, tail swinging gently, lower lip hanging and quivering, hind leg cocked. And I felt the same.

Being with the stallion in particular, it became clear that he could only engage with me if there weren't other, more pressing things that demanded his attention, like a rival in the pen across the hillside, or a mare in heat, or a group of wandering herd members that had gone over to a meadow behind the hill across from his paddock, escaping his vigilant eye. How could I ever get him to pay attention to me? I despaired of ever connecting with him with that ease that horses around him commanded. We did our round pen work at liberty, which meant he had a clear choice of whether to engage with me or not. He would often turn his back and gaze out at the herd or race around the pen ignoring me, keen to connect with the horses outside and to run with them.

As I gained more experience in reading him and as I was at the same time more connected to what was going on in my own body, I learned to accept the flow of his attention and disconnection with me, as the demands of the herd became more pressing. At the same time, I learned to listen to what was going in my own body and to be clear about this, before I entered his paddock. He did not mind if I was upset or joyous over my day, if I had a knot in my stomach, or was filled with a lightness of being, as long as I approached him with clarity and awareness of my own frame of mind. His attention came and went; it was as simple as that.

I learned to read the signals he sent and evaluated what he could and could not do in the moment. When his focus was on me, the smallest signals had the desired effect – often it was enough to think of a trot and he would fall into one. However, if his mind was elsewhere, then the same signals would have little effect and it was necessary to get his attention back before we were able to communicate again. To get him to be with me, I needed to calmly enter his pen, breathe, be in my body, aware of what I was feeling so that I could observe him more accurately and gauge what kind of signal would get a response from him. I had to come to terms with my own uncertainty, and trained myself in quiet confidence.

Ala taught me a new understanding of the flow of connectedness and separateness in human interactions, and to read the signals more accurately in order to understand the depth of each interaction. This flow could be disconcerting, as I wanted for connection to be a permanent state once I had reached it, and it was a challenge to wait out the disconnect with quiet confidence.

This happened in a different context when I decided to reduce my role in the company that I had co-founded, and to hand over parts of my job to new staff. Wanting change for myself deeply upset the dynamics of the office, as I was no longer willing to "do whatever it takes". There were many moments when I felt that disintegration and chaos were on the horizon as we restructured the company. However, having experienced with Ala that there is a flow between connectedness and disconnect in life, and the fact that I had learned to live with uncertainty, gave me the skills to see this through beyond the chaos and change. It also helped me to connect more deeply with this special animal. By accepting that he is what he is, and that he did not need "fixing", we became closer.

One day as I arrived at the horses' place, Ala stood by his gate, full of anticipation, the head dipping up and down rhythmically with impatience to be taken out for a walk or ride. He knickered softly as I approached, and I felt calm and with him in the moment. He was easy for me to read and connect to at these times, his language clear and without confusion, and it made me feel clearer and more aware of our purpose together. Having this connection whenever it presented itself, reinforced my desire to look after him as best as I could. I knew then that I had to make him my horse. That way I would be in charge of his situation, his care, his rides, and his future. He needed special care not only because he was a stallion, but also because of a major injury at age four. The day the sales contract was signed stays forever in my mind, as I remember the joy and anticipation.

As the months and years went by, Ala taught more clearly what he thought and expected: the quick trot for which I had not asked when we turned away from home at what he thought should have been the end of the ride, ears pinned back when he was cinched up too quickly for his taste, scratching the ground impatiently when it all took too long, and always wanting to fulfill his deepest desire, to be a stallion in all his capacities, to sire again.

Then one day, it was time for him to sire another foal after the other two that already formed part of his current herd. I felt confident that I was able to take on the responsibility associated with letting the horses create a new life. Rosie, the strawberry flecked grey mare, with a lineage as impeccable as Alakaset's, seemed the best choice.

The trainer and I set off on another ride, up that hill on one of those rare, very hot coastal days, not a cloud in the sky, the air still and vibrating with heat. It was mid afternoon and the dirt road up the first hill felt steeper than usual. We continued on a path meandering up to a far meadow, at the other end of the property away from the herd, which had not followed us today because of the heat. Once we reached the meadow, we dismounted, took off saddles, halters, and bridles, and let them loose. There was no fence for miles to keep him in or to keep her out. They were free to do whatever was their desire, and it was their desire to graze and graze and graze while we sat in the shade of a large oak tree sheltering us from the sun.

Was she in heat? Maybe it was over already? Or had he lost interest in her and would rather enjoy a rare chance to graze freely? Who knows, we speculated. We waited a little longer, thinking they might not have noticed that there was nothing to keep them from breeding.

As we sat, the heat crept into our bodies. We finished our water bottles and got ready to tack the horses up again when we saw Ala approach Rosie, sniffing her gently, then snorting, as he arched his stallion neck. She softly whinnied back. The heat spread their excitement all around us as he reared up and bred her. It was almost too private a moment to watch, I thought from my human perspective, but the horses could not have cared less. They followed their instinct and concluded what they set out to do.

Seeing this act before my eyes made me feel embarrassed and excited at the same time; a powerful moment at the creation of new life that most of us probably do not get to be privy to. And the horses reminded me of the naturalness of this all as they repeated their breeding act after a grazing break.

The sun dipped lower and I felt the cool air from the ocean rush up the mountain and fill the horses' manes. They were done with grazing and breeding and after an exuberant race around the meadow, allowed us to catch them, tack them up, and put on their saddles. We got on and rode them back home, with the stallion occasionally bursting into showy strides, arching his neck, but always respectful of the rider on his back.

Facilitating and watching this act of creation made me realize the primal power behind the sexual act, something that I had never really considered. What struck me most was how "natural" the horses were in this undertaking. Everything had its place and even though breeding was not a daily event, it still had its place in their universe, along with other activities like grazing together or riding up the hill together. This natural order of things, combined with the primal power, took my breath away, and it taught me that this is also the case for human sexual interaction: it has a natural place in our life like all other bodily needs, but at the best of times it also transcends that physical situation by creating a unity between two separate beings, a coming together in full connectedness, when a true "we" is created.

Again, the stallion showed the way by reminding me of the natural order of things that form our lives, and that this too is part of the flow of connection and separateness. It is only if we truly are in our bodies and in our heart that we can become connected with others and can become one with another.

Ala, more clearly than other horses that I have come across, is a master at the language of the body. He is his body, and shows me daily that in order to reach depth in any relationship, whether with horses or humans, I too need to be in my body – not just in my head and in verbal language, but in nonverbal language, facial and bodily expressions, feelings, and physical presence. He teaches with great clarity when I am disconnected from him and our lives run parallel without interconnecting. It is this flow of connection and separation, so deeply exemplified in a stallion's existence that directs life.

Birgit Weskamp, The Spirit Horse, Mixed Media 2008

Up The Hill

This is how it started,
foot in the stirrup,
up I went,
and into the saddle.

He moved under me,
and his movement moved my body,
flowing up the spine,
through the hips as they mirrored
his moves up and down,
and I swayed from side to side,
wobbly, uncertain of where to put my body on his.

He seemed huge at just over 14 hands.
What have hands got to do with size?
I did not care,
he was huge as far as I was concerned.
My body, scared and excited at the same time,
and then I felt like I was sailing through the air,
all this movement without me moving a muscle,
just relaxed.

And he settled into a gentle walk,
then a slow trot,
and I bobbed about,
ready to fall off.
This really was not comfortable, I thought,
as I felt my sitting bones hit the saddle.

Up the hill we went,
escaping the words that overwhelmed me.
Up the hill we went,
past oak and manzanita trees,
past loose horses milling about,
and calling out to mine.

Up the hill we sped,
faster and faster,
and I could only stay on his back,

this my first horse,
by being connected body to body,
this small brown horse with the big heart
and the desire to do what was being asked of him.

Up the hill we went,
and the vistas opened up:
we saw the bay with the ocean and the mountains
while he moved gently under me.

Up the hill we went,
and I was scared.
I felt the fear in my body
and located it in my belly,
but the gentle movement dissipated it.

Up the hill we went
and into a new life,
a new adventure,
which filled me with excitement,
all so new.

Up the hill we went
into a different state of being in my body
that I did not even understand fully on this my first ride.
I never even realized what had happened.
I did not see that this was more than an adventure,
more than a new sport,
more than just movement.
This was my introduction into a different way of being.

Up the hill we went
and we came down,
both of our lives different.
Up the hill we went,
and I never wanted this to end,
this connection body to body.
Up the hill we went
into a new life.

Up the hill into my body,
and this was what I needed

after a life of living with my brain, the intellect, the talk,
seldom clear enough to connect,
descending into the darkness of the body.

Just this abyss,
the black hole that haunted me at night,
into the abyss of drugs and pills and suicide attempt,
and I was not at home in this life
and it haunted me
and threatened my life with its regular presence
like clockwork.
As if this body of mine was not to be silenced
and wanted to be heard.

My body refused to be the pillar that my head rested on
as its crowning glory,
screaming to be heard and noticed,
only to descend back into the abyss,
haunting days and nights with its diffuse and chilling presence.

And I wanted to find a way out of this imprisonment,
as more intellectual challenges piled up into this my life,
teaching in an environment
that did not care what the body needed,
at the same college where Stephen Hawkins taught
whose ravaged body hardly supported his brilliant mind.
Was I turning into just a head, all head and brain and thought?

Deep into the darkness I sped,
down into barbed wire and more darkness,
and it was hard to be myself and not doubt my abilities;
and back down into the darkness
as the clock kept on ticking,
down there with fear and immobility as companions.

And when I came back up,
the world still looked the same,
and I still had a hard time connecting
to whatever emotions were filling my body.

But now there was a different kind of darkness,

this darkness in his eyes,
the eyes of this horse that took me up the hill,
eyes full of depth and trust,
eyes that shone with hope,
eyes that reflected the world back,
eyes that showed me me.

And there was no longer darkness that threatened,
but darkness that showed off the light in his eyes,
and his gaze penetrated my body, my heart, my soul.
Did I even know I had a body and a soul?
Just one glance showed his depth and he just gazed.
Then a blink,
and his gaze wandered off my face
to follow the movement of the herd,
breaking his connection with me.

I felt bereft and abandoned,
and followed his gaze,
watching the herd move on to the next meadow.
He stamped his foot impatiently,
and asked to follow them,
while he strained after his favorite mare in heat,
snorting and showing off his arched stallion neck.

He reminded me that I am not a horse,
and that we flow in and out of connectedness.
His eyes had been vast oceans of connectedness just a moment ago,
when I had felt seen,
and being seen, felt myself.
I felt my heart expand and connect with his,
just for that moment.

Then he moved on
and reluctantly I moved on with him,
watching him,
breathing with him,
and walking with him,
as I felt disappointment and sadness fill me
over the loss of our eye connection.

Moving on with him, the sadness dissipated,
moving on into the earth
that we were stepping on.
Suddenly there was the joy of stepping out together,
side by side,
following his need to be with the herd.

He did not mind me being there,
and when I stopped walking, he stopped too.
There was this moment of awakening
when I looked into his eyes,
and felt the depth of his being expressed in them,
with all the trust and wisdom
that he had gained in his life.

It made me deeply happy to have this gaze see into my eyes,
and it penetrated, where years of intellectual endeavors
– so foreign to my deepest nature –
had never penetrated.

His gaze was like a warm torch,
like the sun's rays that melted ice
that lightened up the darkness of years accumulated.

As the miles took me away from him
as I floated over the clouds in a plane,
like I imagine his spirit floats Pegasus-like,
He was there with me in that moment
because he was my feelings and my heart
reaching a depth of heartfelt connection
that gave a new dimension to my life.

Up the hill we went
and we came down,
both of our lives different.

My thanks go to my husband Robert, who has been with me on this journey with love and encouragement, and to my horses Alakaset (Ala), his daughter Alshama (Ali), and my newest horse, the master teacher Kairos.

About
Birgit Weskamp

After having spent 30 years in an academic and business environment, Birgit entered the horse world upon turning fifty, without realizing the impact this would have on her life: a reconnection to past artistic interests that had lain dormant during years as a university

Photo by Donna Stidolph

teacher and company co-founder, and an introduction to the physical and spiritual world that horses inhabit.

Born in Germany and educated at Freiburg, Glasgow, and Hamburg Universities, she concentrated her studies on theatre, directing plays, and also teaching modern languages. During her time as a lector at Cambridge University, she explored human interaction as an intellectual endeavor, trying to understand how breakdowns in communication are expressed in the artistic medium of the theatre. This culminated in a doctorate in interaction theory. However, it was not until she observed and experienced the power of the nonverbal and bodily language of the horses, that a more complete picture emerged for her.

Birgit enjoys expanding her interaction with horses by transforming these into artistic expressions, both through language and images. As a mature student of all things equine, she feels fortunate to have a forgiving and patient teacher in her first horse, the Arabian stallion Alakaset. Birgit is a devoted amateur who acts out of love for horses.

Birgit can be contacted at alakaset@yahoo.com, and her website is www.horseworldjourneys.com.

Opening My Heart to Trust Again

By Caroline Rider

Brandy was aging quickly and losing weight every day. His shaggy winter coat could no longer hide his ribs, and the life in his eyes was beginning to fade, as they were often glazed over, sunken in, and dull. He was beginning to show signs of a neurological disorder, as he was dragging his left-hind leg and was unable to swish his tail. He struggled every day to walk and graze, and his appetite began to wane.

As painful as it was to watch him wasting away, I didn't believe he was ready to leave me. Although I could see the light in his eye decline, I could also see his eyes long for me as he softly nickered, embracing me with a hug between his chin and chest, holding me each time for what seemed a lifetime. So, I waited and with each passing day, held my breath, as I knew his departure would leave me feeling devastated and alone. Little did I know that with his passing I would be faced with a range of emotions that would leave me mourning for years.

My dad was also having a difficult time watching Brandy's health and life energy diminish. He loved Brandy, sharing a daily ritual and bond with him, having taken over being caretaker in my absence. Both my Dad and I had spent a huge part of our lives with this amazing creature who lived in our back yard. When I got married and moved away, my dad needed Brandy as much as Brandy needed my dad. They both filled each other's hearts and lessened the pain and reality of my absence.

Dad's way of dealing with the pain was different than mine. For him, finding another horse to become emotionally involved with was the answer. So, he set out, unbeknownst to me, to find another horse for us to love. He did not know that his efforts would backfire on him, as I wasn't about to let another "love of my life" into my heart, especially before my beloved Brandy had departed.

I was living in Washington, D.C. with my husband the year Brandy died. We would visit my parent's farm every month, just so I could spend time with him. Because of the difficulty of seeing him age so quickly, my time with him was very uncomfortable for me. It wasn't so much the physical condition of him that bothered me. It was the sadness I felt when I left him, a longing within my heart that I just couldn't escape. A joy and peace within that I had let go of because I didn't believe I could ever find those feelings again.

Detaching myself from him when I moved away became easier and easier. However, I had no idea at the time that leaving Brandy behind would feel as if I had left myself. I had defined myself through the relationship I had with my horse. The "real" me felt so comfortable when with him. I could feel at ease while feeling vulnerable, expressing my feelings and raw emotions with total abandonment. Being with Brandy allowed me the emotional space to be who I needed to be and in time develop the courage to trust myself, my intuition, and to find my inner voice.

Knowing the real me well had not always been the case. Speaking my mind when I was young was so difficult for me. Not only was being a teenager uncomfortable at times, it was especially challenging because I was constantly trapped within my head, making any effort to reach outside myself almost unbearable. The only way I felt comfortable communicating was through my artwork and then with my horse. Only in those times did I feel present, centered, and grounded. Any other time I reached out to communicate, I would become self-conscious and easily overwhelmed with my emotions. This overwhelming state eventually led to me shutting down, experiencing intense panic attacks that would last for years.

I've often reflected back to when I was young – the very first years I began caring for Brandy in my back yard – and I can vividly recall feeling joy, excitement, and hope. It was a time when my young mind "believed" anything was possible! I wasn't yet "trained" by adult life to worry or care what others thought or projected. Being young and naïve allowed me the opportunity to remain innocent, honest, and open toward all things and views. I remember it being easy to see the core of what truly was, and staying present long enough to actually inhale and embody the many moments of connection I felt with all things. The time I shared with my horse allowed me to feel safe, magical, and "one" with another being. In the time we shared together, I could see and feel my horse giving me his time and heart, unconditionally.

As I grew into my teens, I had a different awareness. The present was no longer as magical as it once had been. It was more about self-preservation, my way of escaping the inner turmoil and angst of my emotions and thoughts. I had changed and with that change I had left behind a very important part of myself: my inner voice. What changed me wasn't just one occasion, but a multitude of instances, over time, that just seemed to beat me down, leaving me spinning out of control within my mind, frequently switching to auto-pilot, so I could check out of class and check out of reality.

The pain and confusion of that time was so great that I couldn't function well at school or at home, disassociating myself to the point of feeling numb, isolated, and indifferent. The only association I had with any feeling was when I was with my horse. His presence allowed me to feel safe and connected to a place I trusted and was too scared to open to others. Our time together allowed me to "be" and not think. In that emotional space, I was able to experience my feelings of joy, promise, and unconditional love.

As long as I reached out my heart to Brandy, he would consistently prove to me that I could trust him and that he was dependable. Our moments together were like magic; he would speak to me with his eyes, ears, and body. His attention to me proved over and over how real our bond and connection was, often showering me with daily knickers and hugs that made me giggle with glee as he pulled me into his chest. I can remember brushing him and admiring every contour of his shiny red coat and muscled body, his soft eye and perfectly pointed ears, and most of all the way he would turn to look at me while I was admiring him. Those were our moments of heart-felt connection and oneness, and with each sharing, our acceptance, trust, and respect for one another grew, deepening our bond, our love, and our friendship.

Before long, our rapport made it possible for our riding to feel as one. Long summer days were spent being together, connected through movement, riding without a saddle and bridle through 500 acres of hay fields, and grazing for hours while catching up on reading. We often went swimming in a near-by pond, resting only long enough to share lunch together. I was his herd and he was my soul mate.

With all of these memories of Brandy, the day my dad found another horse for me to love was a stark contrast.

The day was cold and wintry as I drove by myself down to my parent's farm. Dad was unusually excited that I was coming and it hadn't dawned on me why, not even when I pulled into their driveway that overlooked the barns and paddock area. As usual, my eyes quickly scanned the area, searching for sight of Brandy. I didn't see him at first, but did notice that the paddock was closed off from the pasture, where he usually hung out. As I walked up to my parent's back door, my dad could hardly contain himself, "Did you notice anything different in the paddock?" he asked.

I gently pushed my way by him to unload my things and then turned around, quizzically replying, "No?" I really wasn't in the mood for guessing games, as my mind was always on Brandy when I got to my parents' farm. I was always so excited to see him and spend time with him.

I peered around Dad's shoulder and out the back door for Brandy, and what I ended up laying my eyes on was this pretty little red bay Arabian. Immediately I refrained from even acknowledging this new horse. I just couldn't believe it. How could he? I immediately became irritated and could feel my body tense as I fought back rage and confusion. I was enraged because it appeared to be an utter dismissal of my horse's existence, as well as my request not to get another. All of which was compounded by the confusion over the many emotions I was feeling that I was so afraid to express for fear of losing my temper and exploding. I did contain myself long enough to utter something to Dad that reflected my surprise and dismay. No matter how I felt at that time though, I couldn't keep back the excitement as we went out together to meet and greet "our" new horse.

He was an affectionate little guy, named Legend. He had no problem making his way over immediately to say hello. It was clear too that he had instantly become fond of Brandy. I remember the two of them exchanging breath and soft knickers across the fence. It was interesting to watch the connection between them as Legend became very excited, strutting back and forth in front of Brandy, often stopping just long enough to touch him. It was easy to see, by the way in which they greeted one another, that they were instant friends, making their transition into a herd dynamic easy and peaceful. With this, I opened the gate and watched as Legend flogged Brandy with attention and affection, almost knocking him down in the process of his excitement. Before long, Legend was inseparable from Brandy, grazing beside him, often playfully nipping at his hind end, and laying down next to him during the warm, sunlit winter mornings.

It was interesting for me during this time as I was emotionally "hands off" when it came to taking any interest in this little Arabian. But, I just couldn't shake him – literally. He would follow me everywhere and come running to the fence when I pulled into my parents' drive. Mind you, he only saw me about every 4-6 weeks. And between being who he was, extremely open and loving, and my Dad's constant attention, he was becoming quite the back yard companion.

I soon became fascinated with him. I couldn't shake myself from thinking about him when I was away. He had this uncanny way of endearing himself. His eyes reminded me of an old soul. While they were alive with expression when he was feeling affectionate and flirty, they were also soft and vast when he was listening.

While I spent much of my time just hanging out with him, adoring his sweet and playful nature, I began to think about what it would be like to ride him. It was a train wreck waiting to happen! I had no idea that what I observed on the ground with him, between his playful nature and need for companionship, would indicate his range of emotional intelligence and complexity.

The more time I spent getting to know him, the more obvious it became to me that he was complicated. When he became excited, whether over apples or affection, he had no reverence regarding boundaries, often nipping at me with excitement. It became clear to me how truly "green" he was to training as well, even at the ripe age of eight. I soon discovered that haltering him to brush, and then preparing him for riding, would become a game of head tossing, dodging the saddle, frequent nipping, and cow kicking as I went to cinch the girth. It became more and more apparent to me that this little Arab was a lot to handle, and if I was going to spend any time with him, I was going to need to invest myself between time and my heart.

Legend had a wonderful way of "waking" me up every so often. Just when I was content to be where we were and not invest too much emotional energy, he would surprise me by doing something that would allow me to see the depth of his character – his mind and his soul. Such acts were his constant serenading me and showering of affection. He would show this by his desire for my companionship. Over time, I became more and more aware of what it meant to be chosen by a horse. This little guy really wanted me as I could not go anywhere around the farm, not even walks by the creek, without him running alongside the fence line, literally calling for me with loud, earth shattering guttural screams that only horses in distress make when they cannot find each other.

As I reflect back, perhaps he was calling out to my soul, calling me back to a place he wanted to share with me. But I wasn't ready to let him in. Not yet anyway.

Legend had incredible charisma, too, and while I felt him generate a great power within that often drew me to him like a magnet, I was also intimidated by the depth of the feelings I felt when he would call to me and present himself with such strength and presence. I wasn't able to identify with, or understand, the depth of what he gave then. It wasn't that I took anything he did for granted. I just wasn't open to allowing another being into my heart so fully and with such total emotional abandonment.

For me not to connect with Legend was challenging. He had this uncanny way of appearing when you least expected it, whether in your dreams or right in front of you, peering over the fence at you with alert ears and large eyes. He always seemed to offer himself unconditionally, and was very expressive and communicative when it came to how he felt at any given time. One such remarkable experience was when we had to put Brandy down.

I knew Brandy's time was coming, and when my Dad called me, I heard what the tone in his voice reflected. I vividly remember hanging up the phone as I dashed around, scrambling for my overnight things, my head swimming with so many thoughts and my throat becoming too thick to swallow.

As I drove into their driveway, I peered out the small barn where I could see Brandy huddled in the corner of the stall. Dad met me as I walked over to him and informed me that Brandy hadn't left the stall in a couple of days, nor had he eaten or drank from his bucket. I immediately called my vet, who was able to come at once, and then I began to gently lead Brandy by his chin down to the far pasture where we wanted to bury him.

No sooner had I gotten him out of the stall, than I heard a frenzy of hoof beats racing toward us. It was Legend and he was screaming at the top of his lungs. He came to a sliding stop beside us before he pranced around Brandy several times, ending up behind him, nipping playfully at his flanks as we walked on. He stayed behind us until we reached our location, where he remained close by and grazing. We remained that way for what seemed an eternity waiting for my vet.

This was an incredibly sad time for my parents and me. We huddled over Brandy's body, sharing our tears, each taking time to touch him, caress him, as he lay there for one last time. I remember weeping loudly at one point, only to be interrupted by Legend's actions as he galloped around us screaming out at the top of his lungs. He would then run out to the other horses and then back to us, just long enough to run his nose over Brandy's body, from one end to the other. I had never seen anything like this before except on television.

*

The show was a documentary about African Elephants and how they mourned their dead. The researchers had identified their actions as highly emotionally intelligent. What I remembered most, that was forever imprinted in my mind, was how affected they were over the loss of their friends and family members. They would travel endlessly in search of food and safety from poachers, often coming across the remains of their dead. The footage showed each of them, one by one, picking up the remains, the bones of the deceased, and caressing them with their trunks. Some would even take their legs and rock the body of the recently deceased elephant, almost in hopes of waking them. I was amazed to see how they expressed the depth of their sadness and grief.

With Legend, I could see the resemblance in his actions. I could feel his emotions as he pranced around, screaming out and then galloping off. And, in that moment I felt a heightened energy around me, that passed through me and engulfed me. I remained seeing everything around me, and yet nothing at all, as my senses were on overload, hearing, smelling, tasting, touching, and seeing. The moment seemed to stand still as my senses merged and Legend returned to stand over both Brandy and me. What resonated most within me was the depth of feeling, the calm and stillness within. I had stopped sobbing and remained quiet, listening and savoring. I felt my beloved horse leaving this world and passing through to another, and in that passing, my new horse had proudly taken on his purpose of becoming a lifetime companion and partner to me.

Eventually all of us, Legend included, returned to the barn to watch Brandy being buried. And as we watched, I'll always remember the look on Legend's face as he stood twenty feet from us with his head hung low, his eyes expressing such sadness, his body exhausted with sweat. He returned once more that morning to the spot where Brandy was buried, to walk over his grave and say goodbye before galloping off and screaming one last time. I never did see him return to that spot again, at least not when I visited.

This experience was just the beginning of many incredibly expressive and heart-felt moments with Legend. Every encounter with him inspired me to open up to feel again the depths of acceptance, trust, partnership, harmony, peace, and oneness.

Present Day

I remember the day I "woke up" and finally heard my horse Legend speak to me. He always "talked" to me, nickering to greet me in varying octaves and guttural noises. But this day was different. There was not a sound, but a deep, penetrating silence as my eyes met his and time stood still. It was one of those moments where you are deafened by the impact of what you feel, not by what you hear.

What I felt was a tremendous weight in my feet that not only grounded me to a complete stop, but also knocked me to my knees. In that moment everything within me and around me fell silent as I was rocked within by deep waves of emotion creeping up and into my throat, choking me into surrender as a calm sensation erupted in my body and shot out toward my horse.

When our eyes met, he spoke to me. His ears perked forward and his eyes reached out to mine, full of question, asking, "Did you hear me?"

"Yes – finally!" I replied with my heart. I then stood up quietly and made my way over to him. He leaned into me and embraced me with his body, nickering softly with acknowledgment. At that moment, our souls had met with an exchange of heart-felt energy that filled us with calm, serenity, and togetherness. I was overcome with a sense of feeling light, as if our souls had left our bodies, merging as one in the great abyss of emotion. The sensation lasted only for an instant before I fell to my knees again and sobbed uncontrollably at his feet.

I cried for many reasons that beautiful, crisp spring morning with Legend. The tears I shed allowed me the release I needed and the permission to just "be" who I needed to be, in that moment. My horse's undivided attention and acceptance gave me the strength and courage to feel the deep well of emotional turmoil within me. His unconditional love and non-judging nature allowed me to feel free as I surrendered my heart, giving myself permission to feel vulnerable and to trust another being other than myself. I cried that morning to release myself from myself, too, and in that moment I asked Legend for forgiveness – for I had been blindsided and selfish.

I cried because I was finally able to let another horse into my heart after spending 25 years with only one. I was finally free to not only love another horse again, with all my heart, but to love myself. Remarkably, all of these emotional releases became the beginning of much laughter and amusement, as I began to "lighten up" and not take myself so seriously when working with my horses. I believe this had everything to do with letting go of my head – of who I thought I had to be, and beginning to live my life authentically within. Because of this epiphany, I was able to be present, and "be in the now" with my horse, rather than where I thought we needed to be. Again, my horse was teaching me about the process – the journey, the moment, and most of all the many heart felt rewards of our relationship.

In the beginning of my journey back to horses, there were more times than I'd like to admit that I was either gently, or fiercely, reminded of my agenda. And the day I heard Legend, I needed a fierce reminder of how goal-oriented I was, putting my agenda before my horse, thus losing all sight of what truly mattered… the journey into the relationship.

The day started, as any other day of practicing my horsemanship skills, with on-line exercises. At that point in my life, I was venturing back into horses and full of absolute conviction and passion… at least I thought it was passion. I was reminded that I often put the "cart before the horse" and on that particular day I was well on my way to making my horse crazy!

I used to think that my blind obsessive drive was the same as being passionate about life, but really, it was an insane drive to acquire things such as: status in my relationships, objects, trips, and most of all, experiences. Yep, I needed to be the "topper" when it came to experiencing life. How could anyone feel what I felt and understand life as I knew it. I spent so much time in my own head and convinced that I was special just because "no one had experienced what I had" that I made it my life's ambition to be the only one who could experience life best. And in return, I had turned myself into a very unhappy person who was no longer anchored in what mattered most. It eventually took each one of my horses to show me who I had become, as they carefully revealed to me virtues that I had lost: truth and humility, selflessness, unconditional love, trust, patience, forgiveness, and most of all, the many emotional rewards of letting go.

This so-called passion was becoming borderline obsessive compulsive that morning, as I was convinced that Legend and I were going to achieve 1, 2, and 3 of the program, no matter what. And, as blind-sided as I was with achieving my goal, Legend was equally intent on challenging my intention, no matter how dangerous the circumstances became.

It all started again, as with most working sessions, with me leading Legend somewhere outside of his emotional threshold, or comfort, to work. I had brought him out into my front yard that beautiful, crisp spring morning. I could tell immediately, as we began walking away from the barn and our every day training areas, that he was becoming excitable, anxious. I didn't understand the concept of "emotional connection" like I do today, so while I could visibly see his physical stress, I didn't know how to deal with, or manage his emotions.

As we walked further and further away from what was comfortable for him, I could see his stress escalate. His head got higher, his eyes larger, he began to scream for his friends, all the while looking all around him as if any minute, he might get eaten by a tiger. It was so obvious to me that I didn't exist in his world, and in that acknowledgment, my own emotions began to escalate; emotions that stretched from one spectrum to the other. The most prominent were defeat and disappointment, and with these emotions, I brought to our time together a huge mental block that began to manifest itself around fear and expectation. Fear of failure and the never ending, haunting nag within my head that screamed out constantly, "You should be here by now, accomplishing this and that... What's taking you so long?"

The horsemanship skills that I had been taught at the time certainly weren't helping either of us. But I didn't trust myself enough to stop and listen, so I kept up with the insanity, asking him to perform specific movements or techniques that I was told would eventually bring his focus back to me and help him calm down.

Unfortunately, none of them seemed to ever work with my high-spirited Arabian, who was also too smart for me to comprehend at the time. Instead, the more I moved him around, the more he would escalate emotionally, fueling his ever so charged adrenaline until he was on overload and ready to explode. I had NO idea that he wasn't emotionally capable of handling the intensity of the request. Asking him to move into a trot, or perform specific footfall, like a side pass, was like asking him to jump off a cliff. At least, I'm sure that's how he felt as he nearly jumped out of his skin every time I asked.

This became a pattern for us, and on that morning, I was determined that we were going to conquer this "rut" in our learning and move on. Again, I had NO idea that all this amazing little creature needed was for me to slow myself down, to stay present with him enough so that I could begin to "feel of him, for him, and then together." Each time I asked him out and away from me on my long line into a walk or trot, he would escalate and speed up, change direction, twist and buck, and then look at me with his huge, beautiful, expressive eyes, as if to say, "STOP! Don't you get me, or what works for me?" And, all I could ask myself was, "What the heck keeps happening here? Why doesn't he get what I'm asking? How many timesssssss have we done this exercise in the arena and it has worked?"

We went back and forth with this for a while out in my front yard, under the 40 plus cedar trees. All the while the morning sun cascaded upon us its brilliance. The beams of the early sun were bright as they caught my eyes between the trees, and then glistened over the morning dew. Each time Legend and I moved, I caught another ray of light that blinded me and for a second or two, I was stunned into stillness, as I could not see where I was going. It was in one of those moments of stillness that I was given an opportunity to listen to what my horse had to say.

Being still and in the moment was one of the most challenging areas for me when it came to working with horses. It meant embodying intent. I had no idea back then how to govern my emotions, manage them, let alone what it meant to be congruent and responsible for my thoughts and actions. I had no idea how sensitive horses were, either to what we felt within ourselves, or how our feelings were easily expressed through our body language. It would take some time before I would be able to realize that true partnership and harmony depended upon me being congruent with what I thought, how I felt within, and what my body language expressed at that moment.

So, while my body was asking Legend to follow technique 1, 2 and 3, my mind and heart were expressing something totally different, making my communication with him unclear and incongruent. For horses, this is confusing and for Legend, being the persona he was, this was unacceptable. His ability to see right through me challenged my every request with willful determination, until I became too exhausted to continue the insanity. This left me feeling even more like a failure, perpetuating my mindset and need to make it happen, no matter what. And, the irony was that the more I made Legend repeat the exercises and techniques, the more my heart sank, and with it came a darkness that filled me with a rage that not only scared my horse, it frightened me as well.

Looking back, I believe he needed my mind and heart to be present, just like when I loved and cared for him. When I was just being with him, loving him, and not expecting anything, I was feeling of my horse, and for my horse, thus allowing us to feel together and as one. Because of this experience I would soon learn one of the most amazing secrets to mastering myself and becoming one with my horse – embodying intention. As long as I carried it with me when I was working with Legend, we would remain connected in spirit, in movement, and as one.

On that spring morning, I was reminded once again of where I was and who I needed to be by a horse named Legend. He once again presented himself to me truthfully, and in return I was finally able to hear him speak.

What he gave me then, and continues to give me each and every time I am with him, is a belief in something greater than myself, and with that my heart is always open and listening.

Legend

Much heartfelt thanks and appreciation goes out to my family and friends who share in my dreams, believe in me, and support my journey. And, of course, I couldn't have written this were it not for the love and respect of my horses, both past and present.

About
Caroline Rider

"I believe horses to be incredibly intelligent, feeling and sentient beings. They are my soul mates, companions and teachers. It is also my belief that in order for us to work with horses naturally, we must allow them choice and freedom of expression. When we allow, we are aware and present, opening ourselves, and our horses to all possibilities – opportunities to create and share deeper rapport, bonding rituals, 2-way communication, companionship, play and partnership.

This is a way of being (Taoism) that I practice everyday with my horses, and one that allows me to reach my potential and theirs."

⸰ Caroline

I've spent my entire life around horses, beginning with my first lesson at the age of four. As a young girl, I showed and worked locally for a riding instructor while taking care of her beloved, backyard equine Brandy. It was during this time that my view of being and working with horses began to shift, motivating me to seek a more harmonious way in which to be with them and communicate my requests when training and working.

As an early teen, I spent much of my time observing horses and sketching them in my journals. I attribute my passion for drawing and painting to being inspired by nature, especially the horse in all its magnificence. My desire to learn prompted me to question the purpose of all things and their interrelatedness to one another.

My craving for more knowledge led me to seek out many different philosophies on horsemanship, levels of consciousness, and spirituality. The most influential readings for me were the *Black Stallion Series* and books I found at the library on Taoism, an Eastern Philosophy that teaches the many depths of spiritual authenticity through living in the present and with consciousness. Between reading, sketching, observing horses, and spending all day with my own horse in the summer months, I was soon on my way to discovering what I know and teach today – mutual trust and acceptance are the keys to acquiring true partnership and leadership with our horses.

It wasn't until my early thirties that I was able to support my enthusiasm for horses and re-enter the equine industry, specifically the very well publicized world of Natural Horsemanship. I felt a kinship to the teachings of many of the well-known and leading clinicians and spent much of my time absorbed in their practices while cultivating my own style and approach to Being and Doing with horses.

My Tao of Horsemanship™ Approach to Being and Doing with horses is what separates me today from most natural horsemanship clinicians. This approach combines three core foundations to horsemanship: natural horsemanship beliefs and techniques, classical dressage principles, and Taoism – a way of being and interacting with horses mindfully. My method helps to identify awareness within us that allows for all possibilities with our horses. With awareness comes the opportunity to identify "where we need to be for our horse, when we are needed (timing), and why." This is crucial to creating and nurturing deep levels of acceptance, trust, connection, communication, partnership, and leadership with our horses.

For more information, visit www.riderhorsemanship.com, email crider@carolinerider.com, or call 410-873-2350.

The Magic & Mystery
of the Wisdom of the Horse

By Linda-Ann Bowling

The walls of the prison feel cold and dank. The bars obscure my view, and looking outward I see another drunken brawl. I am 3 years old, and the prison that holds me is actually a "play" pen – an oxymoron, to say the least. Watching the chaos and feeling the pain, I promise myself that someday I will find a better place to live, wondering how adults can seemingly take such pleasure in the bottom of a bottle. This is my first and most vivid memory as a child. It spurned me on over the next few years, as every thought went into keeping me safe and hidden.

In the meantime, my safety depended on my ability to read who was trustworthy and who was not. This self-protection helped the refinement of my empathic gifts and kept me whole. While someone can ravage your body, they can never take your soul. By the age of 12, I left that "prison" behind and went on to build a new life for myself. It was not until years later that horses would find me, and I would at last begin to feel...

It was during my mid 40's, on a cool, crisp day in October while out on a trail ride with my sister and the ranch wrangler, when horses actually found me. I did not dream of horses as a young child. I was too busy dreaming of a safe bed to sleep in, warm food in my belly, and something other than the smell of a man's alcoholic breath on my body. This is a story that is aching to be told, a story of horses and the opening of my heart.

During a beautiful fall day when the meadow was alive with the songs of birds in the distance, we rode toward a treed area, two parts separated by a creek. I remember the thought, "Oh good, we'll clippidity-clop through the water and be on the other bank!" In the flash of an instant, I was on the other side. As I turned in my saddle to tell my sister to hold on, she, too, was already on the other side. Both of us had managed to stay upright in the saddle. Our horses seemed to take great pleasure in jumping from one side to the other, and somehow I imagined that the horses were sparing no expense in teaching the city slickers how to ride.

In the moment that I reached the other side, an electric shock moved through my body. I felt tingly, as the supposed innocence of my youth returned for a brief few moments. With newfound energy flowing through me, I decided to hang back from my two riding partners, and started to talk, whisper, whistle, and sing to my horse. Curiosity filled me as I began to wonder about this animal that carried such lightness, and yet held such an incredible feeling of power and freedom. Maybe I could learn something about how to restore this within myself. This awakening was shared with no one that day.

Over the next several months, as my fascination with horses continued, lessons became my passion as I became a diligent riding student. Several months passed before I finally became a student of the horse. After reading the *Tao of Equus* by Linda Kohanov and attending one of Linda's weekend retreats at the barn where I rode, the feeling of exhilaration and unconditional joy that comes from playing with a horse began to find its way into my heart. Thus began my journey into the unparalleled and unmistakable wisdom of horse.

A Miracle Named Rio

To learn about this work and integrate horses into my life coaching practice, I needed to hang out with the horses, to understand their ways better. My vision was to lease an older, "bomb-proof" dark-colored horse (in those days I had no idea what color, breed, etc. were all about – forelocks were lovingly called "bangs"). This would truly be a horse that I could trust to take me on safe trail rides. However, the universe was busy giggling behind the scenes, because this was the furthest thing from what ended up becoming reality.

Each day when I came to the barn, I caught sight of two grey horses, each wanting some attention. I continued to walk down the aisle without giving them a second glance. After all, neither of them fit with my vision for that dark-colored safe trail horse. One day, my trainer asked me if I would take one of them out for a walk. I emphatically said, "No. I told you I don't want to get attached to any other horse until mine comes along."

There was a twinkle in her eye as she laughed and said, "Actually, I think he already has." I scoffed and grumbled as I decided to halter up Rio, one of the grey horses, to take him for a walk. Evidently Rio had decided to win my heart, and he was working very hard at it. The only trouble was,

Rio was the spookiest horse I had ever handled. He actually made me laugh each time he would shy away from some new thing that happened to find its way into our path. A blade of grass, a dandelion, a piece of wood; heaven knows what he thought the porta-potti was.

Many days I would come to the barn and we would fall asleep in the sun. I would perch on my chair that leaned on the outside of the barn while Rio towered overhead with his head balanced on my head. All the horses would fall asleep and the chorus of snores, including my own, competed with the yawning of the barn door as it moved back and forth in the gentle summer breeze.

One day in particular I remember just falling into a peaceful and blissful sleep, only to be awakened by Rio's head landing with a thud on top of mine. We all woke up at the same time, each horse looking down the line to see which culprit had assaulted our sleep time. Rio seemed rather embarrassed, with a look on his face like, "Hey it wasn't me!" as all the horses proceeded to put their pajamas back on and continue their afternoon siesta. I just sat there giggling, thinking what a motley crew we must look like, and then laid my head against the barn wall and went back to sleep.

With the help of my incredible trainer and coach Christa, I worked extensively with Rio on the ground to help build his confidence (and mine) as I learned to navigate him safely in the round pen. I taught him how to keep his head and energy low to the ground, to stay focused and to continually find his feet. As it turns out, Rio is what we call a "wind horse". He is light-footed and sometimes loses a sense of being connected to the earth. He was also quite disassociated from being handled roughly before he came to our barn. It was quite the long road to recovery to bring him back to himself.

Over the next couple of years, Rio taught me about patience, taking baby steps forward in our learning, and most of all how to keep my heart open. Actually I had no choice because he continually made me laugh through his playful antics. I never knew what might be around the next corner, and goodness knows I had better figure it out or I might be holding an 800 lb Arab in my arms!

In the midst of all this learning, Rio decided he wanted to be front and center with my coaching clients. He would continually push his way into our coaching conversations as centering activities were constantly interrupted by nips on the shoulder. Rio was clearly eager to show my clients how skilled he could be in helping them navigate their challenges. Rio proved particularly adept at helping women who carried a lot of stress in their bodies. In fact, he would nip at them continually until they learned to bring their breath into their bellies, drop their shoulders, and set strong, healthy boundaries. Only then did he feel safe.

After conquering all the horse-eating challenges and things that go bump in the night, my trainer and program partner decided that Rio was finally ready to participate in one of our Horse Guided Learning workshops. Needless to say, I was skeptical to say the least. While I knew Rio had come a long way, the big white building that shuttered in the wind, amplified voices, and horse-eating shadows did not produce the most conducive "coming-out" celebration. As Rio came into the arena with one of our Safety Support Advocates, my breath caught in my throat and, like a nervous mother, I actually think I stopped breathing. The woman who had chosen Rio for this particular reflective round pen process had formed a special kinship with him and would not be deterred from time with her new friend. Little did she know…

What happened next can only be explained as the magic and mystery of horse wisdom. As Rio's learning partner stepped into the round pen, she began to confront the feeling of fear in her body. The warmth of the sun on her was lost in the internal struggle to stay connected to the earth. Her heart connection with Rio began immediately as she stood in the middle of the round pen – there was no touching – at least not with hands. Her heart began communicating her pain, and Rio turned to face her. As each person watched, he became totally focused on this woman. As they moved closer to face each other, Rio and this woman appeared to be consuming each other. There was no sound, no licking or chewing (by either of them!), just the rise and fall of each breath. At least ten minutes went by with no movement as they stood transfixed and transformed by each other.

Rio's body appeared to have grown exponentially at the same time the woman appeared to get smaller as he now looked down into her eyes. I could see the tears welling up in her eyes, and still he stayed focused. Tears did not break the surface, but the emotion was palpable for both of them. Those watching were not breathing for fear that this magic might be broken. Eventually Rio put his head down, licked and chewed, let out a sigh, and the lesson was over for the moment.

When the process did finally end, Rio's learning partner said, "I felt as though I was looking into the eyes of God. I felt naked, stripped down to my soul – I could hide nothing. My vulnerability was undeniable, and I could not break the spell. The feeling in my body was like being raked over hot coals, while at the same time, I felt the cooling sensation of an ocean breeze. I cannot explain it, but this horse looked inside me and found my pain; gently and gracefully he began to hold it, show it to me, and move it out of my body. This is like nothing I have ever experienced. I felt totally exposed, and yet somehow safe."

The connection that was made by Rio and this amazing woman that day was the way horses communicate telepathically when the channel is open and available for healing. This horse knew how to tune into the place where this woman held her pain, and reached in as purification and cleansing began. The most incredible thing occurred after this program, as Rio became a different horse. For six months, he never spooked. He was still curious and playful, but had incredible confidence and a peace about him that began to sustain him. This was truly some coming out party!

Witnessing the coming together of two souls as each offered healing to the other is both a blessing and an honor. This rite of passage transcends any human/horse relationship as space is held for whatever wants to emerge. This soul-connection allowed me to develop a deeper understanding of myself as I imagined that it was me that day in the round pen – standing naked before this wisdom horse. What did I need to let go of? What was holding me back from tending to my soul's divine purpose? How could I serve the world in a bigger way? What pain still lingered in my heart, continually surrounding me with fear and shame? These are questions that Rio has helped me to find in those special, soulful moments when all things somehow seem to come together and I am in perfect harmony with myself. Most of all what I have found with him is the wonderful healing of laughter.

Prince of Light

He is my white horse, my Prince of Light, who came to me on a stormy November evening in 2006. When he walked off the trailer, he held himself with a superb dignity. However, he was several hundred pounds underweight, his coat matted with fecal matter, his tail hidden beneath mounds of mud, manure, and other unidentifiable things. Yet beneath it all, I could see the stateliness of this horse. He walked out into the pasture and turned to look at me, in the midst of a freezing, cold, and rainy night, as if to say, "What took you so long? I have been waiting and Princes do not like to be kept waiting."

He is a Lipizzaner, and his age unknown. We suspect somewhere between 35 and 40 years old. He does not live his age. He is vigilant when there is any herd movement and he is hopelessly in love with one of my mares, Melody Joy. She tolerates him at best.

Prince's story is one that he does not like me to talk about. It is beneath him to hear the words. He was left to starve to death in the field and was sent to auction. He came close to being sold for $150 to a man who would turn him into meat or some other less than dignified specialty. He was rescued by a woman whose soul cries out for the atrocities of what man has done to these precious beings. Perhaps one of the reasons I feel so connected to him is that I too remember a hungry belly, one that did not get enough food to eat as I went to bed each night with the sounds of Johnny Cash playing throughout the night. I never knew whether it was safe to leave my bedroom to see if the party was actually over for fear of being discovered as another "available" woman. Most nights I just let the music play…

Prince of Light came to me in my dreams many nights as my body broke out in a cold sweat. I could not name the horse, or know where he would come from, but my heart knew he was there waiting…

In the three short weeks that Prince was with me, I quickly learned that no gate or barrier would hold him captive. He is a freedom horse and will not be fenced in. He took several fences and gates out before we all realized what he was trying to say. He now roams the property freely, *and* has learned to respect the humans in his life when they say, "Back up – no more gates can be replaced – you may hurt yourself or another horse, and that just isn't going to work!"

He has gentled himself as he has re-built his trust, and we all know better than to move his mare too far from where he can see her. Someone once said to me, "He has to learn to be separated from her!"

I asked, "Why is that? Is it because we as humans have decided how he will deal with his emotions? He has earned the right to have us work around some of his idiosyncrasies. In fact, I honor them. At his age, we can certainly give back to him what was taken away through many years of working hard to carry "greenhorns" on his back. While I recognize a day might come when he and MJ might be parted, we will deal with that when it is here. In the meantime, he gets to choose!"

Prince's story took a turn during that first month with me. It was a Saturday and I was moving through my morning ritual. Hop out of bed, check the horses out the window, make my morning tea, and head down to the barn to hear the soothing sounds of breakfast. This particular morning as I looked out the window through the continuing torrential downpour, I saw Prince writhing on the ground. Soaking wet, covered in sand, his blanket wrapped around him, I raced down to try and figure out what was happening.

It didn't take me long to see that he was having a severe colic attack. His eyes were rolling back in his head, he was kicking at his stomach, and his life force was weak. I cut away the soaked blanket, which felt like it weighed more than him. I sat in the sandy paddock in my pajamas with his head in my lap – trying to get him up had failed. As I sat holding his massive head, tears streamed down my face, and I told him I was really mad! "We have so much work to do, you and I. There are so many humans to help heal. I have waited a long time for you, and you for me. If you are giving up, then go, but do not be dramatic, it is too painful. This isn't just about you; it is also about me and what we have planned to create together. We are bound to each other." I brushed the sand away from his face, kissed his head, and rubbed his stomach. By now, I too was soaking wet.

My neighbor came rushing to the fence to find out if there was anything she could do to help. I moved to the fence and told the story about how I had found him and how sick I thought he was. As we stood and cried over the fence together, I said, "Well, if he's going to die, he better just get it over with. I'm cold, hungry, and frankly quite mad!" She laughed, I laughed!

Within a few seconds of the laughter, I felt his heavy head on my shoulder as if to say, "What's all the commotion about?" He was up. I walked him around in the pouring rain, both of us looking like two drunken sailors in a stormy sea.

The vet came within a short time and thus began several weeks of helping to bring this stoic power horse back from the brink of death. He was poked, prodded, intubated, and every other thing that would help the vet restore his health. I learned more during that time about injections, white blood count, starvation, colic, mouth ulcers, and digestive issues than I had planned to ever know. It took us several months to stabilize Prince, to find the right mixture of food that would help his stomach heal and that he could chew (he has almost no back teeth – they had literally rotted out of his mouth).

Today, Prince is a healthy, vibrant, self-righteous, huge energy horse who knickers when his favorite vet comes (how many horses do that!). He is deeply grateful to be on this planet and to continue his work with humans. He even allows us the occasional ride and true to Lipizzaner style, he knows how to move under saddle. He is truly a sight to behold.

Prince's gift to the world is his ability to seemingly understand the English language, and to hold space for the two-legged clients who choose him. He is wise, beautiful, and powerful beyond expression. Prince chooses to engage with women who lost their sense of power in the world. He holds them until they will stand tall, and *will not* let them go until they claim their rightful place in the world. He will stand at the gate blocking the way out until he feels the energy and flow of each woman who chooses him as teacher. He is insistent that they get this feeling in their body before he will relax and let them move out of his teaching space.

Prince has taught me about how to hold healing space, to embrace possibilities (especially when others thought it was the end of the road for him; "he's old, let him die" was the message from one vet during his severe colic attack), and to stay connected with my authentic self. He is a powerful force, gentle yet strong, and has helped me be whole again, to step into my power. And when I forget, he is there gently nudging me, a soft nicker reverberating from his mouth. He is the one I come to when I need that reminder – his strength and character is a sustaining force in my life and in the herd.

He does not tolerate drama from the humans in his life, as he is the only one who has earned that billing. Prince of Light is a force to be reckoned with, except of course when he lifts his leg like a dog for a good old belly scratch!

Genevive, a King's Love Affair

I am transported to another time and as I hear the breath, I leave my body. When he is finished with her – he rolls on top of me. My mother cannot protect me as her drunk-induced sleep holds her hostage. Is this the ultimate betrayal – what is a mother's role if not to protect her child? I do not blame, I just stay hidden.

My tears fall onto the black horse, called Genevive. Affectionately known as my crying towel, she expertly guides me to the place in my soul that longs for healing. Her coat is well practiced at soaking up the salt and the tears. She does not mind. She wraps herself even closer to me and just waits. The tears become cathartic now as they come from a place deeply buried. I look around and see the abundance of the light from the stars and the moon. There is no struggle, no mind thoughts. There is a feeling only of tiredness that envelops my body, and my mare shivers and shakes it off. She turns to look at me with mournful and knowing eyes. She understands the feeling of being taken, of being violated without her consent. The life of a PMU mare has killed her sense of self. For years, she stood in a stall connected to a tube that collected her urine that would then be sold to develop drugs for women in menopause. Side by side, she and others knew no life except the inside of a barn, tubes, people, and confinement. No earth under her feet or sun rising or setting to keep her health in the rhythm of nature. There is a deep sadness as I hold her and tell her we are now both safe.

I whisper to her in a voice that she seems to understand, "No one will ever take either of us again!" We move away from the holding, and stand apart. There is only peace that exists between us now as we share this expansive moment in time as old things fall away and new things are illuminated. She knows… Her head bows and she glances at me once again with a peaceful recognition that we are joined in a way that will transcend the travesty of a three year-old, a twelve year-old, and now a woman in her 50's who has been called by the horses.

Coming full circle with these animals called horses, I am brought back to myself so many times. Witnessing incredible miracles of healing, unhorse-like behavior that sounds like it comes from fairy tales, I feel complete when in the presence of my herd. They are continuous reminders of what it feels like to be an animal of prey – to be hunted and consumed by others.

Together we have built bridges to the human soul. We have opened the hearts of hundreds of people, mostly women. We have learned that there is no shame in tears, in sadness, or in grief. There will be power beyond what I can imagine when the world discovers the wisdom of the magnificence of horse. Horses are helping to put us back together, to expand our consciousness, build authentic community, create connection, and most of all, to love self unconditionally in honor of our own human spirit.

It is through the wisdom and unequivocal place of non-judgment, unconditional love, and surrender that the horse is waiting to help humans heal. With deep gratitude and humility, and as a catalyst for new possibilities, I stand wide awake in life, in conscious awareness to be the light that shines so that others can find their way. Let the healing continue… one horse, one human at a time! As I ponder my "for the sake of what is calling," I hear the herd breathing in unison and gently holding healing space for those who have lost themselves in the prisons of their own experience. Will you answer the call? If so, when?

Photo by Kristina Belkina

Genevive

I have so much gratitude to my husband, Gregas, who has helped to make this all possible. He helps me intend a new future for this world, one human and one horse at a time. My sister, Donna - Prince's human auntie; Faye, my right arm; and my friend and neighbor Dani. And, of course, the horses, as they stand in the foreground of my heart reminding me to never give up.

About
Linda-Ann Bowling

Imagining my life without horses is hard, although as I describe in my story, they found me not so very many years ago. I did not go to school with the horsey lunchbox or have them embroidered on my socks. I did not dream of riding bareback through the meadow on the back of a black Arabian, as many women who come to me for coaching describe. Instead, the

Photo by Kristina Belkina

calling that is here today is one that fuels the fire in my belly to go out and share the magic and mystery of the incredible being called horse.

With the love and support of Barbara Rector, Ann Alden, Lisa Walters, Christine Cole, Linda Kohanov, Christa Miremadi, and Eliya Finkelstein, I have found a way to fill the void that has lived so long within me. Unable to express sadness and pain, my horses have helped me find my voice. I no longer apologize for the tears, and I can wholly support other women as their tears find them. I can embrace the goodness that lives in all of us as the horses remind me that there is beauty in each of us – waiting to be discovered.

For the past five years, I have been able to share horse miracles with hundreds of women (and a few courageous men) through my life coaching practice and heart-centered learning programs. Leaders have learned what it means to be vulnerable, to ask for help, and to fully embrace "beginner's mind". Teams have played, laughed, and genuinely connected with each other as the horses expertly guide them to new places and new ways of being a team. Executives have hugged horses, learning how to communicate their vision with clarity and power as the horses stood shoulder to shoulder with them.

Most recently we have expanded our programs to include women healing from cancer, women of domestic violence, addictions, and soon to be launched, a school program.

As an international speaker, award winning Master Coach, facilitator, and healer, I continue to be humbled by the greatness of those who find their way to Healing Heart Sanctuary to participate in this work. You are the gift to the world, and it is through your healing that I too am healed.

Unbridling Human Potential, equine-imity – learning life and leadership skills through the way of the horse continues to hold the sacred space of possibility that the world will answer to the call of the horse! This is my dream.

To learn more, visit my website, www.UnbridlingHumanPotential.com.

Rekindling the Spirit:
A New Horizon of Hope

By Mary Elizabeth Meyers

Linda was passionate about her life with horses, and she was fortunate enough to have money to support three very well bred horses and travel the U.S. to compete at Three-day Eventing. My job was to help school her in dressage, oversee the health of her and her horses' well-being, and prepare her for competitions at the international level. I enjoyed working with Linda because the welfare and safety of her horses came first. Linda would not put her horses in harm's way for the sake of a competition or just for the need to ride.

Linda was of short stature, light-bodied, and very determined. Dressage was not her forte, and before I began working with her about the nuances of developing a relationship with her horses, she was experiencing more "downs" than "ups". She had decided to step back and look more closely at where the holes were in her training and re-evaluate the state of her horses' health.

This particular winter was predicted to be harsh. Linda decided to move her horses from the bitter cold of northern Idaho to the warm desert of Arizona for the winter. The sandy soil would be far better to train on than the frozen tundra of northern Idaho. Linda loaded up her three horses and headed to Arizona. I had agreed to meet her there and coach her for her first competition of the season.

When Linda met me at the airport, she enthusiastically began telling me about Dante, a Dutch horse that was for sale. Knowing Linda had been having second thoughts about one of her youngest horses for competition, it didn't surprise me that she was searching for another horse.

"Linda," I asked, "did I hear you say he is seventeen, two hands tall?"

"Yes," she replied with an infectious laugh.

"OK, then, please do tell why you think you would like to ride and work with a horse that seems to be the size of a Trojan horse? Does he come with a step ladder?" I queried, chuckling out loud. Linda laughed once again and then told me that he just seemed like such a great guy.

The next morning, Linda picked me up early and we drove to the ranch where Dante was being boarded. As we arrived, my eyes were drawn to the beauty of the effervescent green grass that shimmered in the morning sunshine. The rust colored mountains along the horizon contrasted the lushness of the pasture. As I turned away from the view of the mountains, I could see the barn and outbuildings, their outline organized and in metered lines in opposition to the irregular, natural beauty of the rust-colored mountains.

Linda walked us out to the pasture where Dante could be found. His outline appeared to curve gently from the top of his head and neck over his back. From a distance, the bright bay gelding looked in good flesh. As we approached, I could see he was every bit of 17'2 hands tall, with a large frame and big bones.

As I listened to Linda relay Dante's history to me, I began stroking the soft musculature along his neck. As she continued to talk, I kept an eye on the gelding. I could see his eyes were distant. As I stretched out my hand toward his muzzle and brushed it gently against his long white whiskers, neither Dante's nostrils nor eyes flinched, his gaze fixated on the "ghosts" in the distance. He made no attempt to connect.

Moving my focus further up his body, I could see irregular white hairs along his back where the end of saddle panels had made contact with his spine. Linda took a closer look, walked around to the other side, and affirmed there were similar markings on that side. These markings were obviously from a saddle causing friction and pressure that results in the loss of hair in those areas. White hair usually indicates a significant bruising of skin and muscle.

"Poor saddle fit," Linda commented.

"Yes," I replied. "And it must have been quite painful to him." As I ran my hand around the shoulder area, Dante noticed me massaging his spine. He dropped his head and then bobbed his head up and down, signaling to me to continue. Before I reached out to stroke him again, a sense of emptiness and withdrawal swept unexpectedly through my body. Instinctively, I knew I needed to step away from Dante to protect him from the swell of hopeless feelings that were consuming my body.

My meeting with Linda came on the heels of experiencing the most tragic loss of my life, the death of my son only months prior to coming to Arizona. I was just at the early stages of being able to feel anything. Day after day an empty void lay in front of me. Barely able to function or raise my head out of the endless sea of grief, everything in my life seemed to be in conflict. I was questioning my life's purpose and my purpose with horses.

In accepting the work with Linda, I hoped to refocus on my work with horses. The prior few years I had shifted from being a classical dressage trainer to physically and mentally rehabilitating horses. Owners that had traumatic experiences and lost all their confidence, or were seeking more than just a training regimen, were beginning to seek my services.

Hearing the soft echoes of Linda's voice as she spoke to Dante, I slipped my hands into the pockets of my jacket and stepped away, not wanting to touch him again. As I stopped massaging, he turned his gaze toward me, pleading for more interaction. But, I was unable to respond. I couldn't give more to Dante, as the interaction reminded me how empty and broken my heart was from the loss I had suffered.

Deciding to prepare him for a ride, we put on a beautifully hand-stitched leather halter. I stayed behind the big fellow as Linda walked him from the pasture toward the barn. His strides were slow, and his attitude about going toward the barn sluggish. After a few more strides, the pace picked up slightly and I could see by looking over the top of his rump that his hind legs were moving stiffly and unevenly. One hind foot was clearing the ground and the other hind hoof was catching the clumps of dirt and grass.

As we secured Dante in the cross ties, we heard the sound of a diesel truck approaching. A very large cloud of dust swirled as the driver turned the truck around in front of the barn. After the dust settled, a tall man, wearing a beige cowboy hat, emerged from the truck.

Linda introduced me. "This is Dan. Dan has been working with Dante."

Immediately, Dan asked me, "Will you be riding Dante?"

I said yes, and at the same time noticed how the gelding stepped back away from him, lowered an ear, and gave Dan a cautious look.

Dan explained that he had been working Dante in the round pen. He didn't say much when I asked what he thought about the white hairs on his back. He was not sure if they were there when the horse came to him. All Dan knew was the owner was afraid of Dante. Dan said that the owner had brought him to a dressage trainer in Scottsdale and that after a short while, Dante had started rearing with the trainer. Dan had initially worked him at liberty in the round pen and then the last two weeks, riding. The owner had been out a few times to watch him work with Dante, but she was still too fearful to get on and ride him herself.

Dan turned and moved toward the opposite side of the barn aisle from where Dante was standing. Dante softly began to chew and stand with one hind leg cocked. I asked Dan, "Has Dante reared with you?" Looking down toward the wooden floor, Dan's eyes turned slightly away from me and then momentarily toward Dante, before he answered, "He hasn't reared since I have been working with him."

I looked at Linda and asked if she really thought she would be interested in buying a horse with the most dangerous and unpredictable behavioral problem that a horse could have?

The sunlit room cast a shadow across Linda's body and increased her height to be much more than what it really was. Although the illusion made her seem taller, I was again reminded of her small stature in relationship to Dante's tall, powerful body. Strong-minded and deeply determined, I sensed that if Linda's heart was set on buying this horse, she would be in the right place to give Dante a second chance at new life. But would Dante choose Linda to be his partner?

We placed the saddle that Dan suggested we use on Dante's back. The saddle was too wide for Dante's withers and appeared to be putting excessive pressure on his spine. The saddle was not appropriate.

After positioning the saddle on Dante's back, I asked Linda to remove the saddle. She gave me a look that questioned why we weren't going ahead with what she thought we had planned.

I then asked Linda to lead Dante to the round pen. As we walked in, Dante began to become rigid, and each time Linda asked Dante to move, he resisted. "We need to let Dante show us what he knows about this environment and expectations. We want to know what he has to say about being in here and what he thinks about us being with him." Out of the corner of my eye I saw Dan sit down on the bench nearby.

Linda removed the halter and she and I stepped back away from Dante. Standing in the middle of the arena, I could see that he expected us to do something. We just stood and waited for him to decide what to do first. As we looked on, Dante walked around the pen, never looking toward us for an invitation to come closer. Dante seemed to want to keep his distance and did not show any sign of being curious about us. As I took a few steps toward Dante, he immediately turned away from us and cocked a hind leg. I asked Linda to walk over and put the halter on. Then I said, "Let's go out to the field and work with Dante out there."

Dan had a surprised look on his face, and said, "Are you sure you want to take him out there? He's been known to bolt and be uncontrollable."

"Have you had him out there before?" I asked.

Dan replied, "Well, no, I haven't. I've just heard that the previous trainer had issues with him running away."

"Thank you for letting me know about his bolting. We'll be cautious and go slowly while out in the field."

Linda led Dante to the large, manicured field as I followed with the equipment. I noticed the worried look begin to dissipate from the gelding's eyes. The worry lines above his eye became relaxed and less peaked. Lowering his head, Dante's rigid body began to soften and relax and displayed a renewed level of energy. As we moved around the field and spent time walking with Dante, signs of acceptance began to appear. He was opening up. Dante began to sniff our clothing and nuzzle our hands. Linda grasped a handful of grass and offered the fragrant food to Dante.

"Linda, did you happen to notice Dante's worried look when Dan approached him at the cross ties?" I asked. Linda was surprised that she had not noticed the gelding's behavior. "My purpose," I said, "is to keep him away from Dan. I really feel like Dante is threatened by him. We won't have Dante's focus on us if he is watching and worrying about Dan. The combination of Dan's techniques and the round pen may be creating concern for Dante. If we want to see more of what this horse is about, we need to take him away from the pen, which has created an expectation. Out here in the field will be a safer environment."

"First, we are going to check out a few areas of his body that I can see are troubling Dante. This could explain why he is behaving the way he is."

Slowly running my hands over his spine, I could feel inconsistencies and irregularities in his spine and lower back. As I ran my fingertips gently along each side of his back I could feel that his spine curved a few degrees over to one side and then back again. Dante's spine was not a straight line from his wither to his croup. When I attempted to check his reflexes in the girth area, he reached around and tried to take a bite out of my arm. No way did Dante want me to make any contact with his girth area. Expecting this reaction, as I had experienced it with many other horses that had been hurt in the girth area, I stepped back toward Dante's flank to avoid his sudden, tense response. Ears pinned and showing signs of aggression, I remained calm and observant of Dante's behavior.

Linda looked quite surprised and concerned over this reaction. "Why aren't you punishing him for biting at you?" she asked.

I continued to keep an eye on Dante and positioned myself behind his shoulder so he could not reach any part of my body with his mouth. "This is Dante's way of telling me something is wrong and that he has pain associated with the girth and the girthing process. Just because he's been ridden before doesn't mean that it's been pleasurable for him. I want Dante to show me where he is in pain. Biting at me is just his way of showing me what is troubling him; it's his way of communicating. If I correct him when he bites at me then I would be telling him to be quiet, don't do that, which translates into, 'Don't show me'. It's very conflicting to the horses when we don't allow them to express their emotion. How else can they communicate with us when they are disturbed in their body or with what we are asking of them?"

Dante stood quietly, ears flicking back and forth listening to our conversation. I continued to stand near his shoulder as he turned his head to the left and tipped his left ear backward as to acknowledge that he was agreeing with what we were discussing.

I'd been waiting for these indicators that he was feeling less threatened about his body. Finally, he gave a deep, long sigh and a long-awaited sneeze with loud blowing coming from his nostrils. His head shook, eyes blinked, and then he gave a very large yawn. Dante's eyes rolled back into his head, filling out the indentation of the socket above his eyelids.

Lifting his head up, Dante rolled out another very long yawn that showed off every incisor, molar, and tonsil. "That's got to feel really relaxing and soothing to him. To me, it's like after having a really emotionally intense cry," I said, as I began yawning.

Linda asked, "Is he letting go of his stress?"

"Yes," I replied. "Dante feels relaxed and safe in this environment, including our presence with him."

Once Dante knew we were speaking of his health, he began to blink, chew, and shake his head and neck. I stepped back away from Dante and allowed him extra space and time to process his environment and absorb the stillness and freedom of just being. Out of the corner of my eye in the distance I could see Dan, the seemingly tall cowboy leaning on the pipe fencing, his hat pushed back off his forehead, now appearing to me to be much smaller in stature in my mind.

With Dante in an environment that allowed him to relax, I was able to get a better idea of areas of Dante's body that could be troubling him. Keeping my fingers together, I gently pressed over the muscles along the spine again. The first time I had felt the muscle, it seemed as though I was stroking a "tightly strung" violin string. This time, the touch of my hand was met with less reaction.

Pointing to Dante's shoulder, I asked Linda to gently press the softest part of the muscle. She did, and as soon as she did I said, "Now, touch his back and feel, if you are able, the difference between the muscle on the shoulder and the muscle on his back, right where you would sit. How do they compare?"

Reaching up again to touch his back and then again to the shoulder, Linda looked at me with wide eyes. "Oh my gosh! The muscle on his back is so tight that the skin seems to be stretched like saran wrap!"

"Yes," I replied. "The softer muscle on his shoulder is exactly the way his back muscle should feel: soft and pliable, without tension. Now feel the tension around his poll. Can you feel how tight the muscles are surrounding his ears and just behind them?"

"Yes, I can," she replied.

Linda decided that she wanted to at least have a short ride on Dante. We placed the softened sheepskin pad directly on his back and then Linda's lightweight black saddle. I watched carefully for reactions to saddling Dante. He seemed to be following our movement and was curious about the equipment. Lifting the saddle, I continued to observe whether he was upset by the contact the saddle made as I placed it on to his back. He gave no reaction as he accepted the saddle. Dante continued to stay relaxed as we finished girthing the saddle.

In small steps we slowly tightened the girth. There was more length and a definite shift in the energy of his stride. He seemed to be enjoying being out in the field. Linda looked toward me and commented, "Do you think he would be okay to ride around the field? I'm more confident now that I see him enjoying being away from the barn."

Checking the girth one more time, I gave Linda a leg up onto Dante. Dante stood quietly as I guided my client's leg into a balanced position. It was a long way up there!

Keeping a watchful eye on Dante, I thought quietly to myself that Dante's physique was overwhelming Linda's.

"Sit forward and lightly on his back. Be careful to not sit back too far. Stay forward and massage his neck alongside the mane." Dante stretched out his long, elegant neck almost to the ground. Linda scratched his neck, and then gently sat down into the saddle.

Dropping his head even lower, Dante looked quite content and I knew at this point that we could motivate him and have an opportunity to check out his gaits. Wasting no time, my client confidently raised her hands and gently gathered the reins. I was getting no indication that Dante was wanting to rear or bolt. His expression seemed without worry, present, and most interested in being out in the lush green pasture.

A woman approached from the barn. As she watched Linda and Dante, she introduced herself as the owner of the handsome bay gelding. She commented on how surprised she was to see her horse being ridden out in the open.

The owner discussed Dante's history openly. "I purchased him at the auction in Holland. I fell in love with his looks and presence. My impression was that he was further along in his training than he actually was. I realized right away when he arrived in Arizona that he was too much horse for me."

Listening to her, I felt she was being genuine and trying to do the right thing for her horse. She continued to describe how much she wanted to give Dante a chance to heal and overcome his fears.

It was the perfect time to talk with the owner about Dante's sore back and other issues in his neck that might be causing the rearing. "By the way, I spent some time going over your horse's body and found some issues that are concerning to him."

A surprised look came over her face, "What do you mean areas of concern? Do you think he is lame or has a sore back?" she asked.

"Well, I am not saying he is lame, although I notice when he is moving at the walk and trot his strides are uneven, causing a pattern resembling a slightly uneven four-legged table. The four corners of your horse are not balanced. Three of his legs are compensating for the shorter one. The shorter, hind leg has less thrust compared to the other legs. So, we are seeing a shorter stride that could appear to be lameness, but is really not lame in this case. It could be that your horse's body is sore from compensating for the crookedness in his body. Does this give you a picture of what could be going on with your horse?" I asked.

"I'm beginning to understand why Dante has been so uncomfortable and how he has been trying to tell us he is in pain. He used to be so easy to ride and work with," she said wistfully. "I don't know exactly when things started to go wrong. His sweet demeanor seemed to disappear in a short period of time. I've really looked long and hard for a horse that I could build a relationship with."

I explained to her that many horses are misunderstood because of their behavior. But, behavior is merely an expression of their emotional state, and

I've learned that you can't resolve behavior problems through training.

"What I am hearing is that Dante was once sound, being ridden and exercised without behavioral problems?"

"Yes," she replied.

"I am certain we can resolve these problems if you are willing to give Dante the time to return to health."

"I suggest you give him that chance by giving attention to his body, then we can talk about training. First we need to give his body time to heal, because Dante is in pain."

Enthusiastically, the owner looked toward her horse and then looked at me, questioning Linda's interest in Dante. Inviting Linda over to the conversation, she and Dante calmly walked toward us looking very confident in one another.

"Linda, what do you think of Dante?" I asked.

"Wonderful fellow," she replied. "I have to admit that I do feel like he is too tall and too much horse for me. I feel like I am not the right person for him with his issue about rearing. I don't think I am experienced enough to help him."

Feeling a sense of relief rush though my body about Linda's decision, I looked toward the owner to check her reaction to Linda's comments. She seemed as relieved as I was that Linda would not be buying Dante.

As we began to walk back toward the barn, Dan met us. Linda and the owner were walking together, and I held back to have a conversation with Dan. He looked at me with a very different expression than when we first met. As we walked across the gravel driveway, Dan asked my thoughts about Dante.

"Lovely fellow and a quick study. He's very sensitive, and has problems with the pain in his body," I replied.

Dan looked at me and stopped. "I didn't realize he was in pain. I thought he was just behaving that way because he knows he is big and can push people around." Dan continued, "I can't believe how calm he was with you and Linda. I haven't seen Dante behave that quietly since he arrived here at the ranch. I guess I really didn't understand that he was trying to tell me that he was in pain."

"Many times people misread what their horse is trying to communicate, and many times owners and trainers try to fix things with techniques, when really all the horse is trying to do is say, 'Stop, I am hurting and I can't learn if I am hurting.'"

"I now understand why you went so slow with Dante," Dan observed.

"I've learned a lot by watching you and hope we can meet again."

As I arrived at the grooming area, Linda and the owner were discussing what would be best for Dante. The energetic exchange between Linda and Dante's owner piqued Dante's interest, as though he knew that they were speaking of him and their plans. He stood, watching their every move, his elegant ears shifting back and forth like antennae absorbing all the information about his future.

"We've decided that Dante should come and stay with you so that you can help resolve these issues," said the owner.

"What are your thoughts?" said Linda.

My mind momentarily flashed to the unexpected feelings I had experienced moments before when I was not able to reach out and give Dante what he was asking from me. Most of my life had been spent living and working with horses and other animals, providing for them as a professional and at my home. I hadn't had time to process all that had taken place in those few short moments. Her question sent a swell of anxiety through my body, and I knew I was having difficulty hiding my uneasiness. Hesitantly, I said, "Would you give me some time to think about this? I'll need a day to check in with the barn and see if there will be a stall available."

Continuing to feel uneasy, I knew I needed to allow myself breathing space so that I could make the right decision, not only for my sake, but for Dante's as well. There was a lot at stake for each of us. I knew both Dante and I were hanging by a frayed thread.

***

Shutting the water off in the arena, I hustled to the end of the barn to catch the call I was expecting from Dante's shippers. It had only been a couple weeks since deciding to agree to work with him. As I reminisced about my decision, my heart raced as I questioned if I was truly strong enough to help restore Dante's spirit. On the phone, the driver confirmed that they would be arriving at the barn soon.

Slowly rounding the corner, the large horse van backed into the driveway, barely able to avoid brushing the evergreen branches stretched out along the drive. I could hear anxious hooves stamping around and becoming louder with each passing moment. Nervously, I reached for the pen the driver handed me to sign Dante's shipping papers confirming his safe arrival. As he handed the papers to me, the driver told me that Dante was an absolute gentleman all the way from Arizona to Washington.

I remembered when I first met Dante, his aloofness, always searching for something far off in the distance. Looking upward into his eyes, I said softly to him, "A small window of opportunity will open one day, and you will begin to see, hear, and feel more than just a saddle on your back, big guy." In my heart I knew he would also offer me opportunity to begin to heal from the loss of my son.

I wasn't expecting Dante to fix my life or cure my grief. The challenge would be to remain vigilant about his needs and create an environment that would allow him to freely express himself. It wasn't a priority to ride or train. I was losing my past identity as an "in the box" dressage trainer and was focused on creating new methods to help horses and people overcome their fears.

Deciding to help Dante heal was a step that needed to take place in order for me to find my way out of the labyrinth of my past. His protective nature would surely rise up if I were anything less than being authentic with my true self.

My plan was to work closely with my veterinarian, who specialized in alternative therapy, to provide Dante's body relief from pain by realigning his body. He welcomed my vet's work on his body and as a result, Dante's attitudes about the girth and the painful reaction to pressure on his back became less evident every week.

The process of acclimating Dante to having a saddle and girth was rehearsed many times before deciding to actually ride him. For the time being, I just wanted him to feel as though he was growing roots into the soft earth, and to feel as though there were no expectations.

As I stroked Dante's neck, my hand felt magnetized to his skin, as though he was inviting me deeper into his spirit. I felt I was being given permission to enter his soul where he was holding his deepest emotions and where his spirit was being held hostage. Like a pebble that is dropped into a quiet pool of water and ripples outward, Dante's energy permeated my heart and transformed in a moment my belief in myself to touch and allow my heart to feel the joy of having helped him become free.

Stillness wrapped gently around us and held us contentedly for a short while. Dante's coat took on a shimmer that I had not yet seen. Glittering colors of mahogany and gold glistened under the lights of the arena. He shook his body as though he had just finished rolling in the soft arena footing. Looking taller and more confident, Dante lifted his head and happily turned toward me with his big, watery eyes. This was the peaceful signal that I had hoped to see in him and I felt it resonate through my body. Dante had become present with my intent rather than hiding with fear of what he expected might happen to him.

My eyes filled with tears of joy as the awareness of seeing things in black and white became filled with vibrant hues of rich colors as my inner self felt the transformation. Emotions came washing over me like a gentle wave cleansing the past and clearing my path. My work with Dante had brought us both to a place of healing.

This was the space of time I had learned to patiently wait for while working with horses, especially those who had lost their confidence and trust with humans.

Dante's gifts of wisdom and willingness to hear my voice from my own true spirit showed me that I had found my way onto a new path of self-discovery: that I was capable of being honest with myself and being present with Dante and not projecting my past emotions onto him.

One day, Dante shared with me his story of abuse. I led him into the arena and mounted him, asking him to walk around on a loose rein. Suddenly, I found myself thrust forward, grabbing mane to stay on and not pull Dante's massive body on me. Holding my breath, I managed to keep a firm hold. I felt as though we were never going to touch down on the front end. Just as suddenly, Dante stopped rearing and immediately thrust his head and neck between his front legs and began shaking and crouching down. Feeling Dante's knees buckle, I jumped off and stepped back to look at what he was doing. I'd never had this experience and I was shaken by what was happening before me. "What is this about?" I said out loud. He continued to hold his head down, still trembling.

Gradually, Dante began to lift up his head, looking as though he had awakened from a bad dream. His eyes were gaunt and he looked confused. I approached Dante and wrapped my arms around his head to reassure him. Loosening the girth, flashes of Dan rushed through my head. Abruptly, my thoughts turned to pictures of Dan using force to stop Dante from rearing. "That's it," I said to myself. Dante is sending me pictures. He finally trusted me to show what had happened to him. Dante knew I would not do those same things to him.

After putting Dante away, I immediately called his owner to confirm whether she knew about Dan's training techniques.

Her voice trembled as she confessed that she had seen Dan use a club on Dante when he tried to rear.

Emotionally drained from my experience with Dante, I became irate with her for her dishonesty about Dante's past. She explained that she felt horrible about what Dan had done to Dante, and she felt ashamed.

"Hopefully, I can work this through with Dante. But, it is going to probably take a lot longer time, and I can't guarantee Dante will ever be able to get over this trauma."

My anger fueled my judgment of the owner. Now, looking back, I could have been more compassionate toward her. Had I been as compassionate toward her as I had been with Dante, I may have created a different outcome for him.

No more than two days passed when I received a message from the owner that she would be moving her horse to another training barn. That was it, no explanation. I called her in hopes of talking with her about why I had over-reacted. My messages were not returned.

Dante helped to rekindle my relationship with myself and help restore my sense of purpose with the horses. Now everything was changing. Devastated, I could hardly look at Dante. What can I do for Dante to let him know what is about to happen? Where do I find the courage to convey to him that our time together is coming to an end?

"Wait," I thought to myself, "why do I need to think that Dante's life is going down hill now that he will not be with me?" I can imagine another life for him and let him know that I will always be with him. Wherever he goes, he will know I will hold him in my heart. I needed to let go of him in the physical sense, but I don't need to let go of him in my heart. He will always be cherished, and the wisdom we shared with one another will always be.

Where did Dante go? I do not know. Much later, after we parted ways, I saw Dante advertised for sale by a trainer who sells horses for jumping purposes.

✶✶✶

The pearls of wisdom that horses own are waiting to be harvested if we allow ourselves to be free from our past, and present with each opportunity we have to share with them.

Are we willing to take the risk of letting go of our identity and finding out who we really are in nature? Horses live by their instinct and have an unfettered self-image. Their wisdom and language have the ability to rekindle us with our own spirit and to mirror to us the place in our mind that seeks to be free of its past.

Dante imprinted the wisdom of his spirit onto mine and helped give me the strength necessary to secure the map of finding my way out of my past of grief and sorrow onto a new horizon of hope.

Sir William

Gratitude to my horses and clients, past, present, and future, who have transformed my life. I am truly honored to have Ramtha, the Enlightened One as my Master Teacher.

About
Mary Elizabeth Meyers

With wisdom cultivated from over fifty years of working with horses, Mary Elizabeth Meyers has created a holistic approach to building harmonious relationships between riders and their horses. Creator of Harmonic Riding – Equine Integral Movement (HREIM), Mary Elizabeth has been a leader in the field of equine health, behavior, and bio-mechanics.

Having trained and taught children for over thirty years, an involvement in three-day eventing, dressage, (FEI) competition, thoroughbred horse racing, hunter/jumper, western showing and rodeos, and the creation of a handicap riding program, Mary Elizabeth has had an enriching exposure to humans in action with horses.

Her passion about the health of the horse led Mary Elizabeth onto the path of becoming a healer of relationships between horse and human. HREIM is focused on the health and welfare of the horse's spirit. It is a process grounded in decades of personal study and observation and supported by current research in the physiology of behavior.

Growing up the daughter of a veterinarian in Eastern Washington, Mary Elizabeth was exposed to a daily life of assisting with a variety of animals at her father's clinic, which directly inspired her to create the work that she is currently doing with all animals.

Through Morven Park International Equestrian Institute, Leesburg, Virginia, Mary Elizabeth completed a nine-month Riding Instructors Certification Program. She then moved to Southern California to pursue her passion with horses and become an assistant trainer and teacher with a Combined Training and Hunter/Jumper stable. Eventually, she returned to Washington to continue a career with horses and become a freelance instructor and trainer working with children and adults.

Mary Elizabeth operates her training facility in Rainier, Washington. She is an advanced student of Ramtha's School of Enlightenment, and travels throughout the United States giving HREIM workshops and providing her healing work to all animals and people.

For more information about Mary Elizabeth and her programs, visit www.harmonicriding.com.

Relationships: For a Reason, a Season, or a Lifetime

By Rachel Dexheimer

My wonderful life with horses came to a sudden halt when I entered my first marriage. Moving away from my family, friends, and the three horses that had raised me with love, patience, and discipline, left me feeling void of the meaningful connections in my life. The horses had been my grounding force since I was 10. They had kept me aware of my emotions and provided a safe place for an adolescent and teenage girl to be confused, lonely, and unsure. In the midst of all of the unknowns of growing up, I knew we loved each other.

The day I got married my inner wisdom told me that it would end, by my choice, and badly. It was not the powerful emotion I had imagined for my wedding day and certainly not what I had dreamed of while watching the Love Boat as a child. At the same time, my intuition was clear that this relationship was going to be very important for me, even if it didn't last forever. That was my first glimpse into the idea that relationships can be for "a reason, a season or a lifetime."

Things were okay at first – the excitement of a new relationship, nesting into a new home – I wanted so much to please him. I wouldn't allow myself to think about what I left behind, only what I was creating. When the loneliness arrived, it settled in like a thick, corrosive fog. The new life and marriage tarnished more quickly than I could have imagined.

Our apartment was near a park with horse stables for people who lived in the city. I would often wander through, hoping to catch a glimpse of the deep brown eyes and soft muzzles. I dreamed of escaping into the freedom I remembered in their eyes – to see them in their glory, coats glowing in the sun, heads held high, thriving in life's abundance.

But these horses didn't know freedom. They were cooped up in dark stalls, eyes glazed over as if in a far away dream. I felt as though I shared one of their dark stalls, watching my own life go by and dreaming of something else. Their eyes reflected my own sadness, instead of the escape I sought.

Some days I could feel the warmth of horse breath on my hands. And on other days I couldn't have felt further away and less alone. I found myself comparing my feelings for my husband to that of being with the horses. When cleaning stalls became more appealing, I knew my marriage wouldn't last much longer!

My inner knowing again came forward, telling me the "season" of this relationship was coming to an end. Not having words for that knowing, nor for my feelings, I wasn't able to tell him I wasn't happy in the relationship, and thought it best for both of us to move on. Unfortunately, I held a belief that just being unhappy wasn't sufficient reason for divorce; someone had to be wrong or to blame. I sensed that he would only "let me go" if he found me unworthy somehow. So, I created a way to get things moving.

It never occurred to me that he would try to control me with violence. The explosions were extreme and unpredictable. His systematic patterns of isolation and emotional abuse suddenly made sense – I was alone and convinced it was my fault. Desperate to create some physical safety for myself, I tried everything I could to control and stop the violence. The confidence and self worth I had carefully built in my physical prowess as a tomboy – body builder, athlete, and rider – evaporated. Defending myself felt impossible. The idea that I was the weaker sex seemed absolutely true. I was no longer safe.

The shame of being a woman and my fear of him became so powerful that my jaws ached from the constant clenching. The rest of my body ached from the blows and the assaults. I was in full survival mode, untrusting of everything and everyone. While I now know my connection with the survival part of myself to be a profound source of courage and strength, it didn't feel that way then. It felt like a prison of confusion, guilt, and terror. Strangely, even through the worst of it, I knew the effects were limited to my physical and emotional bodies – my soul was safe and somehow on the right path.

Thankfully, that path included two wonderful friends who saved my life. I am forever grateful to them.

Moving back home with my supportive family brought me some semblance of normalcy, surreal as "home" was. I felt shattered, numb, and unrecognizable.

In addition to my human family, two of my beloved horse friends were there to greet me. Being such a shadow of myself, I don't even remember seeing them for the first time – something that could have been a joyous occasion if joy had seemed available to me.

Less than a month after returning home, our beautiful bay mare dropped dead in the pasture. We assumed that it was an aneurism because there were no marks in the mud, not a sign of struggle – just her cold body on the colder ground.

Damian, as people called her, was magnificent in her beauty, her femininity, and her strength. A bright red bay with a star on her forehead and such delicate features, we renamed her Dainty Dancer. She was written off by most people as being "mare-ish", a "floozy", and a "tease". And, yet, she was the only horse I am aware of that won the Whidbey Island Open 3-Day Event three times with three different riders. She was very talented and incredibly sensitive.

Growing up, I dreamed of having her unfettered femininity and her delicate strength. Instead, I spent my teenage years listening to people's disgust at her boldness, learning to be ashamed of her for all of the things I loved about her. The limitations that people placed on her became limitations I placed on myself. They drove me to further hide my femininity in a tomboy image.

What I didn't understand was that she offered to me so many times, in so many ways, the key to myself, to my own feminine power – a path through my blinding teenage confusion. In her death, she offered yet another opportunity to see that power with different eyes.

Like each time before, I did not see or accept her final offer. I blamed my femininity for making me the "weaker sex" and not allowing me to defend myself from the assaults in my marriage. So, my feminine power was buried as deeply as I could manage. Not only did I blame it for the violence in my marriage; indeed, I blamed it for everything that was wrong with the world. "It is those stupid emotional feminine urges that ruin everything," I thought. And, seeing Damian lying there, there was more than a small part of me that hoped that weak side of me had died with her.

The rest of me felt as lifeless as her beautiful body. The shell of my body was alive, but it felt like everything inside was hollow and dead.

My precious gelding, Joe, was close to 35, had few teeth left, and we knew he wasn't going to make it through the winter. Joe and I had met when I was 12. I saw a Polaroid photo of a chestnut gelding in a field and I was hooked. My parents did whatever possible to fulfill my dreams. So, home he came! He was strong, confident, and athletic, and everything I would be proud to be. His coat was radiant and seemed to come to life in the sunlight. His eyes were bright, clear, and intelligent. Dancing Wildfire became his name. He would try anything, and that gave me courage to try as well. We would fly over jumps and dance through an arena with grace, turning heads and inspiring "Ahs!" I carried his confidence in my heart and it gave me clarity through the confusion of my early teens. He offered me a place to truly belong and I now realize how profound that gift was.

Damian was Joe's whole life – he adored her, and she adored him. He would have died of heartbreak and loneliness if we hadn't helped him along in his transition.

That bitterly cold November day was agonizing for all of us. Joe, being the friend that he was, knew we were upset and tried to comfort each of us. In the moments leading to his transition, each moment of which should have been all about him, he tried to help us. He seemed to be inviting me to remember our adventures – to trust, to choose life.

Those were not words I could have heard then.

The unimaginable – Damian and Joe were both gone within hours of one another. I knelt next to him, a short distance from the once fiery red mare, both now lying silently in the dirt. The yin and yang of my life were gone. And yet, I had no tears. My body ached and I shuddered with pain. My teeth felt as though they were exploding apart. And, then, mercifully, I felt nothing. It felt almost blissful in the surreal moment of looking at the two best friends I had shared my young life with. Whatever came next for me would be without them. Every shred of my childhood innocence left with the rendering truck. I was numb.

While I was away experiencing marriage, I held onto memories of our love. Now, I was back, and they had moved on. One could say that it was "just their time". My truth is that there are no coincidences. Meanwhile, the weight of an un-mourned loss settled across my chest.

That loss remained heavy over the next several years. Searching for ways to lighten the load, I reflected on the horses' clarity, courage, and confidence. Remembering also, their support, encouragement, and love, the emptiness in my life underscored the fact that I had no idea how to be in relationship. Handing over my power to someone else and "pleasing" had gotten me into my first marriage; I knew I didn't want that. So, what did I want my relationship to look like? And, who did I want to be in relationship?

Not finding the answers right away, I threw myself into work. Several relationships with wonderful, loving men fizzled. I couldn't trust them to not hurt me, nor did I trust myself to keep me safe. So, I stayed safely in my prison of fear.

Finally, when I did find love, it was with a very special man whose dedication to his own dream inspired him to live in Los Angeles. That was a deal breaker for me – my spirit would not allow me to even consider moving to L. A.

In the desperate, choking loneliness that followed that breakup, a piece of me was awakened – the part that could feel. The tears were almost pushed from my eyes by the one-ton weight on my chest. They finally flowed freely, for my first marriage, for the passing of my innocence, for the passing of my horse friends – mourning for each and every loss came pouring out of me. For weeks, I felt raw and mushy, with a cotton-ball dryness in my mouth. The tears seemed to melt away the weight of the grief and I began to notice a small flicker of light that walked with me. In clearing away so much pain, there was room for something else – hope.

And, then, I met Dijon. While enjoying a cold winter day at a local barn, there was a horse trumpeting like I had never heard! Rushing around the corner into a small alcove of the barn, everything shifted into slow motion. The earth seemed to shake as the huge stall on the left seemed to drop from the sky like the house falling in the Wizard of Oz. As the dust seemed to settle, the enormous grey animal inside spun from the window to the door to face me. His head was high, his nostrils fully flared, and his eyes locked with mine. Electricity shot through me and I felt my heart break wide open – all the walls that had been built over so many years, softened by my recent tears, blew apart like a well-rehearsed movie stunt.

Both of our hearts were filled with love and joy!

We spent every free moment together. I groomed him until he hardly had hair. We celebrated being with each other. We laughed and played and scratched and loved. Dijon had created a safe place for my heart to open again and for me to trust. And, as he came waltzing in, a shy, unassuming, modern-day cowboy followed. This dear man co-created with me a safe place to share the joy, gratitude, and silliness that Dijon offered. It was a beautiful time for all of us to re-gain some innocence and to simply be loved.

Shortly after, an opportunity to take a stand for my fledgling innocence presented itself through a new manager at work. We had very different opinions on the nature of our relationship. Just when I thought it was safe for my femininity to re-surface, it was again attracting unwanted attention – and in the safety zone I had created at work. The thought of going to work, of facing him, sickened me – literally. Even in the face of emails, voicemails, etc., the company decided that my repeated and consistent

"No's" weren't clear enough.

Here I was again, with my femininity causing confusion and chaos. This time, an authority figure from the company where I had put all my trust, was telling me my femininity was an open invitation to abuse. It appeared that I didn't have a right to say "no" and still wear a skirt. The shame, guilt, and hatred of that feminine power came flooding back, and the familiar prison walls slammed into place. Rather than seeing this as a chance to change my story, I did the only thing I knew how - locked it away – for good this time. I wasn't going to get into another situation like this, ever!

The energy of my inner conflict manifested itself through my physical body. I awoke from a nap one Sunday morning and couldn't walk – my legs literally would not support me. Again, rather than trying something new – looking inside – I went to every doctor in the greater New Jersey area – medical specialties I hadn't even heard of. For seven months, I searched for the answer in the medical community while I supported my recovery with an energy healer, a nutritionist, a massage therapist, a yoga practice, and my dear hairdresser. Not a single doctor could tell me what was happening or why. Being too stubborn to be written off as crazy, I found one last expert. She had been recommended by multiple sources and my intuition told me she would have the answer.

She reviewed my file, asked me lots of questions, checked my pulse and tongue color, only to conclude there was no reason for a person my age to be so sick. Then, she said something that changed my life. "I don't know what your beliefs are, but I feel strongly directed to tell you to stop looking outside yourself for the answer. You have the answer inside and are the only one who can heal this." Time stopped as her words reverberated off the walls. Did an authority figure with a white coat just give me permission to trust myself? At that moment, my path to healing began.

I didn't make it out to the barn to see my beloved Dijon between doctors' appointments. The first time I saw him, I was shocked. His 17.2 hand Shire/Thoroughbred-cross body was gaunt, his coat was dull and thick, his eyes were glazed over, and his gaze seemed far away. His beautifully carved head was low and he barely moved. He acknowledged me, but was uninterested in anything, including food.

As I had been healing in the safety of my bed, my thoughts reached out to him, talking with him, and wishing I could be with him. I was not aware of the impact of the energy exchanging between us. We were so in tune with one another, he was helping me carry the load of my "dis-ease". As I had become sick, his life-force vibration had slowed in correlation with mine. That was a significant lesson for me in energy and its impact on others. To my wonder, as I got healthier, so did he. And, as I regained my confidence, Dijon's showed more brightly in his eyes. In healing myself I was giving Joe's gifts of love and vitality back to Dijon, completing the circle. That opened my mind to the dynamic, energetic nature of relationships.

The Universe blessed me with two more loving men along my journey. Because of the trust Dijon had reintroduced into my life, I allowed these wonderful men into my heart. Like Dijon, they co-created relationships with me where it felt safe to stand in my personal power and ask for what I want. I love each of them, and mourned when each beautiful "season" came to an end.

Then, one glorious July day, I got a call from one of my oldest and dearest friends – my high school sweetheart. As soon as I heard his voice, I knew. That line, "You had me at 'hello'" jumped out of a movie and into my life. His previous relationship had ended and he called to "see how I was."

So began the age of my second marriage, and the true unfolding of my divine feminine. I was now totally safe to explore and unleash that power that Damian had modeled for me so many years before. In her physical absence, it was Dijon that celebrated with me. The more I allowed my feminine self to open, the more vital his health became.

Beautifully synchronistic events brought six other amazing horses into our tribe, forming a remarkably dynamic herd. I had an amazing marriage, a great paying job, wonderful horses, and fantastic friends – and yet, there was something missing. My heart longed to make a contribution to the world – to know and live my purpose with passion.

That longing serendipitously led me to work with a Master Certified Coach. As we explored my purpose, deep levels of anxiety emerged until I felt like I would explode. The only way I knew to handle it, was to call someone and spew it out all over them. That seemed to have worked for the first thirty some odd years of my life – or had it? As my anxiety spilled out, I noticed people didn't want to talk with me as long, I got voicemail boxes more often, and fewer people answered my calls. Even the dog avoided me.

When none of my numbing medications of choice (TV, food, complaining to friends) worked, it occurred to me that the horses didn't seem to be tired of me yet. How many stories had I read about people sobbing away their sorrows in the neck of a horse? And, it worked with Joe when I was a little girl, trying to figure out why the boys didn't like me; I would feel better and, back then was oblivious to the impact on him.

So out to the pasture I went, thinking, "This will be good!"

At first, they were somewhat accommodating. They listened for a while and then moved away. Not feeling validated, I followed them. They would move again. I would follow again.

Over the course of several days, they continued to raise the bar of their expectations for our relationship – the moving away turned into just plain walking away. I got angry with myself for being so pathetic that the horses didn't even like me, and then got angry at them for not liking me. After all, I wasn't that bad, was I?

After a particularly disappointing encounter, I retreated to the couch and desperately wracked my brain for answers. What was I doing wrong? The pain from what felt like a pressure cooker all around me became too much and I finally surrendered – to hating my job, to not living in my integrity of loving what I do, to being an adult and having no idea what I want to do "when I grow up", to selling out to the security of money. Not realizing it was the first step of my new life, I allowed the pain, disappointment, humiliation, and anger to spill out until there was nothing left.

Much later, in that place of empty, exhausted surrender, I again made my way to the barn to feed the horses. My intention was to stay only long enough to get chores done and then go back to the house to sleep. What I got was my biggest breakthrough about how to be in relationship.

The horses were sweet and curious and totally cooperative. Their eyes were soft; they didn't move away – in fact, all of them approached me, one by one. They reached out with their energy and their noses. They nuzzled me, gently blowing their warm breath into my face, sharing space, and then moving away to allow the next horse to approach. As each made room for another, they formed a circle around me and created a deep sacredness in the moment.

I was so tired; without consciously noticing what was happening, I just accepted these beautiful responses. As I started walking back into the house, a message reached me – as gently as the touch of a feather dancing in a slight breeze: "Thank you for not expecting us to take it." As the words settled in, a deep sense of relief washed over me, like a gentle wave of golden light. We had taken a profound step forward in our understanding and communication.

Finally, I didn't need anything from them, did not seek to please them, and was not asking them to make me feel better. In short, I was owning my energy and emotions and wasn't expecting them to "fix" me. I was simply being – and being with them.

And in that still place, the message could get through; they had merely been asking me to take responsibility for my own energy. Just like the doctor in New Jersey, they were suggesting I look inside for the answer, rather than outside.

The horses had been requesting that I respect them, and not rely on them to carry my emotional burdens. Once I stumbled into that level of relationship, I fully embraced it – and I allowed it to fully embrace me. We were evolving together, laying the groundwork for "lifetime" relationships.

I started listening, watching, and feeling into the herd in a new way. What they helped me understand is that each of the horses in our herd has a structure in which they hold their energy (interchangeable with emotion). It is that scaffolding, if you will, that holds their energy in space. It's much like the image from *Dirty Dancing* of Patrick Swayze's arms as he drew out his "dance space" and Jennifer Grey's "dance space". When both parties hold their space, what happens in the middle is magical and miraculous.

I also noticed that not all horses, nor most people, have developed a defined energetic structure around them. They are not able to hold their own energetic space or maintain boundaries. This leaves them vulnerable to absorbing each others' energy and getting physically ill.

The alignment of this energetic structure with the physical and emotional bodies feels like "emotional/energetic integrity" – the structural integrity of being able to hold space and stand in it, and the integrity of recognizing the impact we have on others.

With guidance from the horses, I started utilizing this "emotional integrity" in my human relationships, with tremendous results. People inherently knew I didn't need anything from them and wasn't trying to take anything from them. It felt effortless, peaceful, and graceful. I was more interested in them and felt less need to talk. Most importantly, it felt like I was walking my talk of integrity on a new level. I had reclaimed my power and had a structure to hold it. I felt whole and fulfilled.

I am so grateful that the horses stepped forward and offered their support. After all, if I want to learn Spanish, I would do best to learn from a master. Who better to help me remember the language of energy than those most fluent?

Through their feedback, the horses showed me that when I am in energetic integrity, I feel like a top spinning true and straight. And when I am either taking something on for another, or asking another to take on something energetically for me, I spin off-center – out of control with unpredictable patterns, often falling out of balance.

From this place of emotional integrity, we co-create relationships as whole and equal partners. As peers, our programs reach a level of depth and service beyond my capacity for words. We find joy and bliss in the moments of being with one another that can expand beyond time and space. Our dance steps express the joy in our hearts in each moment, just as horses dance with each other in their herd.

The horses also showed me that I was not in energetic integrity in caring for them – I was unconsciously trying to "take" their heavy energy to "help them heal." Their bodies manifest energetic patterns in the same way human bodies do. They helped me understand that taking their energy dishonors their path and actually impedes their healing. As I stay more in my energetic integrity, not only do my relationships with the horses deepen profoundly, they are vibrant and healthy beyond words.

As I spent more time in my energetic integrity, my Coach and the horses helped me crystallize my purpose: To facilitate reverent connections to the natural world and illuminate the truth of our Oneness. I champion space for vulnerability, intimacy, and deepest truth, inspiring authenticity, unbridling passion, and igniting purpose.

I have heard it said that relationships come for a reason, a season, or a lifetime. As my awareness continuously expands, I am learning the importance of recognizing the difference. By not trying to make all relationships "a lifetime", I more deeply honor all types of relationships with others, both horse and human.

The horses have taught me that relationships involve a willingness to evolve in this energetic integrity. It becomes a dance of life, of emotion, of light, color, and sound. There is no end to the one and no beginning of the other. There is a joy, a flow, and a harmony to the vibrations that support each being, remembering their greatest and highest selves.

The intricate language of energy is what I have come to know as the art of relationship. The horses taught me that when I stand in my energetic integrity, I form deep, authentic connections that nourish me, nourish those in relationship with me, and nourish our world. These types of relationships are the foundation of a sustainable future, whether they are for a reason, a season, or a lifetime.

Dijon, Trumpeting

I am profoundly awed by the generosity with which the land and the animals, particularly the horses, are offering their partnership for our collective good. I offer my deepest gratitude to them for their relentless voices inviting us back to the sacred wisdom they inherently hold. I also offer that gratitude to my dear family and friends for their love, to my beloved husband for more than I yet know, and to Spirit for revealing the truth in every breath.

Back to Basics

So, you have two assignments for this week. Start making amends to those you've harmed and start practicing "prayer and meditation" on a daily basis. Write down your guidance and discuss it with your sponsor or sharing partner. Also bring it with you to the next meeting.

As for the reading, if you turn and turn method at the bottom of the fourth page of the "How to Listen to God" pamphlet:

> "There is a way of life, for everyone, everywhere. Any-
> one can be in touch with the living God, anywhere,
> anytime, *if we fulfill His conditions*:
>
> > *When man listens, God speaks.*
> > *When man obeys, God acts.*
>
> *This is the law of prayer.*"
> ("How to Listen to God" p. 4)

By making amends, you will remove the barriers that have separated your connection to higher power/emotion... By listening to the God in your conscience, you will be given the "strength, inspiration and direction" to change your relationship with your own... and so to recover and we look no more to humanity. We do this by ...

Are there any questions?

122

About
Rachel Dexheimer

Rachel Dexheimer is the founder of EquiSpire™ Coaching and Consulting located in Maple Valley, Washington. Along with her herd of horses, she inspires people to discover their unique contribution, empowering them to create sustainable relationships, careers, and lives in full alignment with their deepest values and their highest ideals.

EquiSpire's proprietary Present Moment Model™ combines the transformative power of human coaching with the profound wisdom of the horse to re-connect people with the power of their own innate wisdom. From that still place of possibility, comes clarity and true empowerment of the self. In this process, the horses act as mirrors to make visible the personal limitations that can contribute to an experience of struggle and lack. Once people see these limitations, they are free to choose what will support them to move forward into their dreams. The results are profoundly life changing, both personally and professionally.

Rachel spent more than 18 years in corporate America achieving "success." From the outside, everything looked as it "should" – wonderful marriage, great job, beautiful farm, and nice vehicles. And yet, on the inside, there was a deep emptiness. She kept asking herself, "I have everything I 'should,' so why am I so sad?" The horses guided her back to her own path of contribution and community where she found joy and deep fulfillment.

Rachel is passionately committed to offering the highest quality programs with the horses as absolute peers and empowered co-facilitators. She continuously engages in her own personal growth, expanding her relationship with the horses, deepening her spiritual practice, and honing her coaching expertise. She is a Certified Professional Coach, Certified Equine Guided Educator, trained facilitator specializing in adult development, and has completed the Level 1 Equine Facilitated Learning and Coaching certification. She is a powerful speaker who inspires people to re-discover the power, magic, and sacred wisdom of nature, empowering them to choose life as a celebration of passion, purpose, and profound connection.

You can learn more about Rachel, her horse friends, and their service offerings at www.equispire.com or email her at rachel@equispire.com.

The Gift of Agility:
Riding the Roller Coaster of Relationship

By Helen Amanda Russell

The ground thunders, dust flying, bared teeth. Prehistoric warhorse of old, his chestnut mass bears down on the little grey, merciless. In the heat of the midday sun, the mask of "gentleman" is off.

Dark sweat appears on his neck and flanks as he ignores the strains of the old joints in his rage to defend the herd from this newcomer. His awkward, stiff old body comes to life in a way I have rarely witnessed. I stand gripped in trepidation, heart pounding, fascinated by the elegance and anger of the process, offset by the nonchalance of the rest of the herd who continue to graze amidst the fury on the periphery.

As I stumble to gain a new life and identity with my daughter, a new partner, and his daughter, the horses model behaviors that remind me of my past. We gain two new members to our family herd, while the explosions of the old chestnut and the new grey reflect our home dynamics.

I watch the process of change unfold in front of me: insecurity in maintaining and protecting the established herd; a struggle in myself to hold the group together; defending against outsiders, the unknown, and any perceived challenge. Fears arise for me and the horses as something new and somewhat disruptive begins to emerge. As I step into new ideas as to how I want to live and have relationship, the children, my partner, and I all bang heads and have our own explosions!

The horses and some much greater power within me, that small calm voice that waits patiently to be heard if I can remain still enough to listen, has driven me to tread on this new, unfamiliar road. The journey has been like riding a roller coaster and becoming a passenger on the ride of my life, past, present, and perhaps future. A series of logjams appear in my life, showing me where I have been stuck in patterns that inhibit new growth.

I scream silently and sometimes out loud as I travel through darkened forests of my mind, face slapped by branches. I delve into shadowy parts of my memories, such as my passion to write, being stymied at a very young age by a pox-faced English teacher who felt that "good old" negative reinforcement – what an idiot I was for not understanding how to construct a proper sentence – was going to spur me into the creative process of writing brilliant short stories. Her assessment drove me further into the conviction that I was indeed a useless piece of crap.

These past recollections pop up at every turn, revealing sunny peaks of new insights, only to dive down again into the depths of the entangled undergrowth of my past. This is not a stroll through a shady lane; this is a ride with extreme shouts of indignation, ugly parts of my family members and me jumping out of the shadows to confront and frighten. I struggle to maintain control of this new household through temper tantrums and teenage manipulation. My family watches in horror and confusion, or joins in the fray. During a calmer stretch, or in moments of hopelessness, family and friends walk beside me, reminding me that travelling the internal journeys of my past takes a lot of courage and fortitude, and to be gentle with myself.

I continue to be guided and pulled in an unknown direction to a very unfamiliar end, with days of soul wrenching agony and nights of absolute understanding of joy when I wake clear headed with new understanding of how to move forward differently.

The horses nudge me to keep walking on this new path. Typically they model resolution in a group dynamic with ease and grace, although at times they demonstrate raw animalistic aggression. It is their instinct to have quick resolution, so as not to waste precious energy that may be needed to flee from a predator.

Slowly they are teaching me key distinctions on how to grow up and have a mature relationship. I have struggled in my role as an adult for over 20 years. My perceptions are based on earlier experiences of being told how to behave, think, and feel, in order to be loved, accepted, and considered a "good person." These beliefs are now out dated and restricting my ability to have mature relationships, with mutual goals and collaborative negotiation, respect and trust for others, and less competition – how not to match anger and frustration with the same, but to find ways of moving into balance.

Competition versus Collaboration

As Copper, the chestnut, gentleman bully, demonstrates in his fury the dominant, aggressive behavior, Flea, the quiet confident lead mare and matriarch, steps forward, closing the gap between the established herd and the grey newcomer, Pine. Simply walking past Copper as he tries to keep the herd separate by using aggressive charges toward Pine and intimidating herding tactics toward the rest of the group so they cannot interact with the grey, she displays an inquisitive approach. Her dark mahogany frame quietly moves away from the herd, gently approaching the little grey nose to nose. Together, she and the grey wander off to a safe distance from the herd. In a quiet, balanced, nonchalant way they go back to grazing. Thumbing her nose at the struggling male trying to maintain the status quo, Flea overrides Copper's dominant attitude, demonstrating the feminine way of collaborating, rather than the masculine of competition.

I envy her. She exudes confidence in such a graceful manner, moving with a grounded sense of knowing. How do I learn this?

As I watch, it is very clear that Copper and Flea reflect different sides of myself. Copper's dominance gets him food and shelter first. However, his aggression is very tiring and mostly ineffective in the long run.

When it comes to making decisions regarding potential threats to the group, Flea steps in and literally walks to the threat and assesses whether there is a need to fight, flee, or go back to grazing. She doesn't waste time or energy vying for the food or shelter. She allows Copper to expend energy where he feels it is necessary, and he defers to her judgment regarding the safety of the herd. Their relationship flows.

My approach to relationship in my family herd is a battleground. I battle for supremacy on both fronts. I want to be in control; I want to make all the decisions. I have opinions about what everyone eats, and how they conduct their lives. I want to be the one that takes care of all of their needs and concerns. I want my options to be the right ones, for all. I challenge any bids perceived by me as a take over, sometimes subtly, sometimes as blatantly as Copper.

As I look at Flea's role, I see that I have lost myself in the responsibility of mother and wife for the past 24 years. My caretaking and organizational skills needed to raise two small children, while running a household and horse farm almost single handed, are now out of balance. How I am handling myself is not appropriate in my new relationship. The children are young adults, passing through at times, causing friction by testing loyalties, pushing and pulling to re-established old relationships with their respective parents, creating unspoken rivalry between each other, challenging the new relationships forming between my partner and I and each other's child.

I am fighting and struggling to break free from the old controlling role. It is a battle within; there is anger. I am stepping into trying new approaches and styles of communication only to then fall back to the comfortable, yet restrictive past behaviors. There are parts of being in that role that are comfortable, reassuring, and rewarding, and parts that I resent and scramble away from with fear and vulnerability.

Shedding the old cloak I have worn that resembles motherhood, I am stepping into something new. For me, the parent role was one of putting everyone else's needs before my own. Now, I am learning how to say "no" and to create new boundaries through authentic power, instead of force, without being the aggressor or victim. I watch myself wobble. It is an evolving process to step beyond what is familiar, and yes, I will step out and back. It is a process of taking care of me now, nurturing those long forgotten dreams and aspirations, letting the child inside of me step into her glory as an adult.

The horses mirror to me what is necessary to move through these changes. They are in the moment, ever mindful of moving to balance as quickly as possible.

My practice is being present with what is now – and not to continue to project old memories of my mother, father, teacher, and all other authorities onto my new "innocent" partner. Rather than being angry and fighting for my own identity and projecting these confinements on him, I stop in the moments of panic when I am feeling the need to defend, protest, justify myself, and instead I sit with the huge emotions that come forward. As I experience these uncomfortable feelings they begin to dissipate. Through this process I begin to step out of <u>all</u> the roles I play for others. Flea is teaching me how to be strong inside of myself.

As I feel less and less tied to the old voices and roles, I notice Flea becomes more physically affectionate toward me. She stands close for long periods of time and touches with her muzzle. She did not connect with me previously when I demonstrated manipulating, ingratiating, temper tantrum behavior. It never worked. In fact, it caused mistrust in her, as it did for me. She would initiate contact and sniff my face and move off, as if she could not stand close for long.

Flea and Copper

Trust and Vulnerability

Allowing our selves to be vulnerable and present enhances authenticity and can create new ways of relating. First, I must learn to trust myself and others again, in order to feel safe enough to be vulnerable and present.

As the sun creeps across the deck, gently warming my body, a soft breeze brings the smell of dry dust to my nostrils. The parched grass crunches beneath my toes, dogs snap at flies. I am taken to the new member of the herd, to learn how to stand in vulnerability.

Pine, "the little grey", is reticent to be touched. As I walk into his space, he stands ridged, holding his breath. I feel my chest restrict in sympathy. He is resigned to my touch, waiting for the moment he can leave, escaping from being caught, although I still can not help but desire to touch his warm body.

When this horse came to me he was almost impossible to catch. He is extremely sensitive and from what I understand, he was handled roughly, with very little patience or consideration for his sensitivity. As a result, he became leery of people and did not enjoy being handled, let alone being ridden. I had spent six weeks approaching him with no intent of catching him, in order that he could begin to trust that not everyone coming into his personal space was then going to do something unpleasant to him.

I had to put a fly mask on him every morning, to keep the nasty summer flies out of his eyes. He would sometimes allow this and other days not. I respected the days he refused the mask and my physical closeness. My patience allowed the beginning of a trusting relationship.

The more I observed him the more I noticed the way he deals with people touching him. When uncomfortable, he stops breathing and disassociates. My response is to stand close without touching him and simply breathe until I see him relax. During these interactions he has tentatively begun to explore touching me, his head swinging around to smell my hands and brush against my forearm.

I understand Pine's hesitation because I too, freeze when the touch of a hand caresses my shoulders, skin on skin. Even if it is a familiar hand. Tension fills my muscles when, really, my body yearns for the tender relaxation.

As my fingers gently rub along the crest of his neck to his shoulders, he lets out a sigh and brings his head around and his lips gently pause on my arm. He is inquisitive. My chilled hand feels the warmth of his neck and I glide my fingertips and nails, scratching and exploring for a place that causes pleasure and reciprocal grooming. His lips move up my arm to my head, he nuzzles my hair, and with expert precision his muzzle explores my bony scalp. I trust his gentle touch that in another second could turn to a casual bite. I have learned to stay present in my body and be aware of the subtle changes (my gut contracting; a sense of unease) that would alert me if he crosses over the boundary I hold.

My fingers entwine in his long silver mane, my body sensing the subtle flinching of his muscles and the holding of his breath that warn me not to push my luck. The little grey jumps away as if an electric shock passes between us. I moved my hand too quickly to brush a fly from my face. The speed of my movement triggered his heightened senses. He lives always on guard, protective.

Yet so close to flight, he chooses to stay and investigate. His bristly nose explores the soft skin of my arm and shoulder, nibbling the strap of my tank top. Tears well up as vulnerability in me opens. My body, too, yearns for the caress of a casual finger, the gentleness of a hand on skin. My body moves toward the affection he offers. My inner desire wants to curl up and be wrapped in the tender arms of a loving soul just for the pure pleasure of touch.

Yet, as his body freezes, mine does too, at a perceived sign of touch being simply a means to an end. In my past I was sexually molested, making my body hyper-sensitive to being touched simply for sexual pleasure for the other party, with no underlying affection. His memories, possibly from a steel bit over his tongue and between his lips, or the panic and explosion of feelings when a girth is tightened around his ribcage.

For me, as a gentle caress of a hand glides across my skin my body relaxes under the touch, yet always waits, returning to not breathing in anticipation of the shift to a different passion and stimulus.

When either of us encounters these conditions, our bodies freeze in anticipation of having to perform, the nurturing nonchalance of touch gone, drowning out any earlier relaxation.

My hand on Pine and my new partner's hand on me in intimate moments, are innocent of the past traumatic memories. The hands glide and bump into the rocks and boulders that block our psyches from allowing new experiences to be had. Held in an old pattern of fight, flight, or freeze, we are unable to stay present in the unencumbered touch of "this" new hand. But through consistent patience a new experience does, in fact, emerge.

Pine leans in to rub his head on me, with mutual contentment. The ache in my chest subsides as I feel his acceptance and trust. My body thrives on the sun's rays, soaking onto the skin and into my memories, allowing my heart to open from the grip of the cage it has lived within all these years. Tears stream down my face as I sit in these emotions, helping the child within to let go of the past and embrace the present day.

Warm breath at the small of my back, a gentle, exploring muzzle releases my body tension and makes me lean into this sensual touch, bringing soft tears of loneliness. Pine sends a quiet request for some belly scratching. As I explore, Bay's huge velveteen body comes to join the healing circle. I feel accepted, loved; one in a group of gentle giants.

Isolation and Rivalry

Still, questions fly through my mind regarding this interwoven family group that I live in: my new partner and his daughter, and my daughter, newly arrived with her horse, Tejabo. Are we all just a group of individuals vying for space and cooperation, with our own agenda, and no common group goal?

We are a very complex group, one with lots of baggage, love, anger, frustration, patterns, beliefs, insecurities, strengths, and weaknesses. There is an assumption that we are working in the same direction. How can we possibly know what another's dreams "really" are? Can we work together to find a way for all of us to have our place in the family herd?

Is the way to true authentic relationship through one's ability to fully relate to others? Can we see our well kept shadow unless we have a reflection? Is this what the boiling pot of relationship stew is really about?

Pine, the little grey horse, symbolizes for me hope and light. He is now embodied in the herd, grazing along side them all. He befriends the dark horse, Tejabo, the other new comer; they graze side-by-side, interdependent, yet never losing sense of themselves. That, to me, is the mystery of their message.

As my daughter and I watch Tejabo's first interactions here, of being isolated by the rest of the herd, his shrill, high pitched whinnying sends shock waves through my body. The intensity of the calling spurs me to leap from my chair and comfort him, to fix the situation for him. Instead, I sit and learn from the fiery interactions, knowing that real change does not come from walking away or removing discomfort, but by finding new resolution, within the uncomfortable emotions that arise.

His presence has even driven the soft-hearted "middle man" Bay – a horse who accepts all – to sense rivalry. As Tejabo is pacing and whinnying he shows signs of an inner ploy to take a female from the herd for himself. Bay, now determined to keep the females, drives him to the outer limits, away from the herd. Tejabo shows signs of compliance. Being alone is more comfortable than the constant threat of attack and pain from one within the group.

Tejabo turns his energy to my daughter and myself and gives us an anxious whinny. We take him to the comfort of his own space and food, in the barn, where he can relax in a familiar, human environment. The beginning of Tejabo's life was spent at the racetrack, where each horse lives in its own individual space and has very little physical contact with other horses, let alone a herd. That is his comfort zone, familiar, and limiting.

Rivalry intentions from the herd and Tejabo's wish to go to the comfort of isolation reveals a similar pattern in me. I feel this reflection coming over me like a tidal wave washing through every fiber of my being. It tastes like metal in my mouth. My teeth clench, my shoulders tighten. It will not be suppressed – it bubbles and boils to the surface, wanting to be released, quenched by tears flowing freely, allowing the feeling to flow out of me. Sitting in every sensation, it wells up, the body releasing the long and ancient story that has to be laid to rest.

Again I see myself mirrored by the herd. Tejabo shows me how. I am always aware of potential threats from the outside to my most intimate relationships. There was always something or someone that was more important than me – siblings, school, other women, career – that seemed to threaten the integrity and security that I was seeking to establish or maintain with mother, horses and ponies, friends, boyfriends, husband. Those moments created a sense of panic, possessive clinging. I feared someone would be taken away from me.

Now I perceive a threat from within my newly formed family group: the relationship between father and daughter that had been well established prior to my new partnership. I feel it gaining strength again. Panic sets in, as I see a pattern repeating itself for me. How I dealt with this familiar sense of being abandoned was by being stoic, stand-offish, refusing to commit totally, feeling the pain and internalizing it, then being the one to initiate walking away so as not to be the one abandoned. The isolation in this pattern created relief. I could control who came near. Ironically, I am ostracising my precious new relationship in an attempt to control and preserve it.

As I sit in this pattern of rivalry and isolation – every man for himself; seeing all others as a challenge, the warrior within me constantly armed and circling, combating all; always having to be right; always having to be above, better than, "fighting the good fight" – I keep trudging on, on my own. I feel uncomfortable, even claustrophobic. The piece of me that wants to hide the little girl who doesn't want to sit in the pain watches Tejabo interacting with the herd. It is revealing – and tiring.

The difference between Tejabo and me is that he will take care of himself within the group, his moments of relaxing interspersed, flowing in and out, taken when needed.

My vigilance is constant. The only way for me to relax and not be constantly on guard is to isolate, alone in a safe place, my space, my house. But that is gone. I am now in a new home with new people. I am conceding to live by their rules, thinking there is no choice, yet really never losing that panic to just be me, never really trusting, never really relaxing. So, it seems my life is controlled by everyone else's moods.

Until, in anger, my quiet voice within bursts to the surface refusing to be smothered, standing my ground. I am the middleman, like Bay. He is willing to go with the flow until the threat comes too close to home. Then an aggression that I have never seen in him boils to the surface. Like him, my pattern changes and I fight for what is important to me instead of walking away and conceding to another.

Balance

Anger and aggression are natural and even appropriate at times. We, like the horses, are animals too. While sitting in those emotions for long periods of time is not healthy or productive, it is sometimes necessary to be in the place of authenticity, acknowledging the anger that arises when we must protect and defend what is truly ours, then find a way to integrate the wisdom of the emotion as soon as possible. Again, the horses show me the way. This is the balance that is beginning to emerge.

The cloud-shrouded mountains sit in the steel morning light, as I quietly walk beside my "bay" giant. As we pad across the damp soil to join the rest of the herd in their breakfast feast, I feel a smile joined between us as my body moves in unison with his, appreciating the moment of connection, alone, together, the anticipated "goal" of food, the level of drive to get there diluted by the heart-felt love between us. It is like a "knowing" smile, of the love between two adults. That they can have silent eye contact across a room amidst the chaos of life, a similar smile in the recognition of each others' love, and stability in a mutual goal (even if it is for different reasons). Bay's goal is to fill his empty tummy, mine to provide that nourishment, the end result is mutual satisfaction, a feeling of peace and belonging.

The whole herd has played an enormous role of reflecting the stages of stepping into a new relationship, so that I can return to those glorious, heady beginnings, the honeymoon stage where we only reflect the beauty and joy of simply being in each other's presence, appreciating ALL of each of other – even the shadowy parts. I see now how some days I set boundaries with huge aggressive teen energy, which has no real conviction or substance; on other days and topics I am as graceful and grounded as Flea in her matter-of-fact, clear messages. Copper reflects the dominant bully in me, who bares its teeth and rears its ugly head less and less.

Pine I resonate with at a deep heart level, the delightful, chunky, Quarterhorse that has no trust, and has been treated with no understanding of emotions and sensitivity. He is starting to gingerly initiate touch.

Tejabo, in his deep, black, electric intensity, hits a profound nerve within me, uncovering a deeply buried level of my past defenses.

Bay walks with me for no more than two minutes every morning, and in those moments I smile and am at peace, my heart open to the tenderness and calm quiet that is literally the breath within him. That is what I connect to.

These moments are fleeting. That is what I am learning to accept. The horses do not see these moments as "better than" the next moment when a birds flies up from a bush causing them to jump sideways as adrenaline shoots through their gut.

To them, what is absolute I only experience in glimpses: this ability to roll with the punches, to go from moments of ecstasy to agony, not wanting to grasp at one and run from the other. This is how they role model, by allowing and being present. The answers are so simple it is easy to blink and miss their subtlety.

The horses always draw me back to my center, that place of balance. They nourish me on this journey. They remind me to stay present in every action of the day. Their physical presence can maim, and yet their vulnerability in perceived danger is what draws me in, day after day, to be allowed to mingle and touch and be amongst this flow, opening my heart, teaching me a new way to roll with the day, when sometimes our own kind seems so bound to diminish and destroy these moments of pure joy and clarity with logic and rational.

Through this enormously tumultuous time, as things have come to a boiling point with egos and tempers flying, there are segments of this ride that can be described as "the darkest night of the soul". The place where it seems like so much has been exposed, and the soft underbelly cannot find a place to crawl and hide, the armour stripped way. I am left unable to move, feeling like the only option is to "throw in the towel". And yet, there is a piece of the infinite within me that smiles at these points, because in the wretched stripping process a new understanding emerges. In those moments, I step into a shaky, newly formed "me", a butterfly emerging from the confines of a sticky, hard-shelled chrysalis.

New life springs forth and resolution is found within our home. As the dust settles, my partner and I find our connection again, nonverbally, through simple healing touch. In the moments when battle is likely to erupt, we stop, reach for one another's hands and step onto the path of companionship, despite all the voices screaming to battle and arm and slam the door closed – or keep the wall up. This is truly opening to vulnerability, letting down the life long guard of "holding my own".

This is an unfamiliar and at times uncomfortable path. It would be very safe to continue down the old familiar path of behavior, with all the destructive tools of dominance, aggression, rivalry, and isolation. But the horses have mirrored the willingness to trust and walk through that fear when every fiber of my body is screaming at me not to.

The harmony and ease in these new moments of connection are fun and rewarding. There is no need to "work at it" or be on guard. It simply is. Now, as my partner and I reach out to each other, it literally reunites our beginnings and reminds us of the knowing inside both of us that had become buried by the stories of the past. We have stepped on the ride together, again.

Sometimes these moments seem few and far between. And then again, the horses show me how to truly believe that the moments can exist in more than flashes, on a richer more constant basis. The secret is that it is a flow, as simple as breathing, like the ocean tide, continuously expanding and contracting.

As I begin to let the old roles drop away, the house settles into a new rhythm. Daughters leave, stepping into their own lives, as I too learn to step into new roles: business woman, author, and teacher; adding new strength and depth as to how to live authentically in every relationship. The best instructor being life experiences, new awareness, and of course the horses.

The lessons of removing the "masks of the past" and standing in vulnerability to begin to trust and allow our strength to come forward and stay present, is truly a gift of agility, taught most profoundly and gently by *all* horses. Stepping on the ride is our choice.

A heart-felt thanks to all the people and horses that walk beside me on this incredible journey, making my life so rich and fulfilling, and enabling me to take the time to share my past, present, and future with the world.

About
Helen Amanda Russell

Helen Amanda Russell was born in the Highlands of Scotland, into a family that has long been interwoven with horses. Helen was drawn to these amazing creatures from an early age, loving the sense of freedom and camaraderie.

Charlie Boy, her pony from the age of 10, was a trusted friend. They spent many hours roaming the heather-covered hills where there were no confines.

From the age of 11 to 17, Helen spent many months at a girl's boarding school, impressionable years, where life-long friendships were formed, held together in the hardships of community living, separated from family and beloved horses

Helen with Pine

for long stretches of time. Charlie Boy's job was eventually taken on by Matchmaker, a strong willed, incredibly brave mare who took Helen riding across country and over fences without hesitation.

Helen stepped into a short-lived career as a secretary. Working in an office and living in the city of Edinburgh were brought to an abrupt halt after a bad case of bronchitis, taking Helen home to the fresh air and mountains – and the back of her mare – to recuperate. The search for a combination of office duties and horses brought Helen to the next step toward her commitment to the horse world.

Finding a job as a farm secretary and a part-time groom helped her bubbling passions to be recognized, and Helen leapt into the training program to become a riding instructor for 25 years with the British Horse Society, and has never looked back, training, competing, coaching, owning, and managing facilities in Great Britain and North America.

During the last 10 years, Helen has expanded her knowledge in Natural Horsemanship. Her training, learned through many of the masters in this field, has led Helen to an entirely new life. Always fascinated by psychology, through observing herself and others in their interaction with horses, Helen realized there seemed to be something that was never addressed: the riders, and their *feelings* and *behavior* on any particular day. The focus was always on making the horses perform, regardless of how the rider *felt*. Intrigued by this phenomenon, Helen searched out answers. During this process, or perhaps because of it, Helen chose to leave an 18-year marriage for a new relationship with her dear friend and companion Ken.

Thus began the journey of self-reflection, and the discovery through working and training with Linda Kohanov at the Epona Center, in Tucson Arizona, of the real gifts the horses have to offer. This knowledge has driven her to develop her own business in The Okanagan Valley in British Columbia, to share her passion of teaching self awareness for every avenue of life.

Helen's herd of facilitators, two of which began their lives in the Highlands of Scotland, take Helen back to her roots and keep her on her toes everyday!!

For more information, visit www.horsepatter.com.

Trust the Horse to Show You the Way

By Vanessa Malvicini

El Dia and the Triangle

There is a ranch an hour southeast of Tucson called Apache Springs, lying in a canyon, almost at the feet of the Santa Monica Mountain Range. As I stepped out of the car that day, I felt a big white shield around me, above me, and all over the ranch. The feeling was very strange and I pulled my head down as a reflcx, as I didn't want to be hit by it. When I realized that it was not a real threat to me, I straightened myself and walked toward the barn. Years later, I realized that horses create these kinds of protection around the people who are living with them. I suppose that it is an energetic shield that only allows into the space what is meant to come into it.

It was morning, yet the sun's heat triggered the plants' release of their sweet perfumes, filling my body with peace and satisfaction. The grass was yellow with some green patches here and there. At the barn, Linda Kohanov, author of *Tao of Equus*, was waiting to facilitate me in a round pen session.

When I saw where we were going to have our session, my wide view, like horses have, became focused. My heart began to push against my chest and blood surged through my veins as thoughts spun out of control in my mind. I was here to have an equine experience. With great effort I focused my senses and calmed myself.

El Dia was the horse I had chosen for that day's activity. He wasn't a horse I knew, but I had a feeling that I wanted to work with him. El Dia was a handsome bay gelding, who apparently was a cowboy's horse before coming to the ranch.

He was trained to hobble, a widely used method to teach horses, donkeys, cows, and other beings to stand still. Many people use it so that, in case an animal gets trapped, it does not panic, but just waits for the rescuer to come. So the animal remains trapped and quiet. That also means that the animal, while hobbled, is not able to move around. It can only stand, staying immobile for long periods. El Dia wouldn't move, even if someone invaded his space, pushed on him, moved around, jumped. Maybe this is what some people would call a "bomb proof" horse. In my view, he was just a horse with no light in his eyes.

As I approached the round pen, I said to myself, "Great! This is part of my search to see if I have the skills to do this work with horses. Linda is looking at me, and this horse doesn't want to move, no matter what!" Then my ego started to accuse me, "You are always the same, you go and look for the most difficult situation you can get into! Who do you think you are? This horse is not going to take one step for you!" My mind's chatter was very lively and giving me a hard time, as I was no longer able to see all the different possibilities that were there for me.

Here I was, a woman who had traveled 36 hours from South Africa to be in that place, and there was El Dia, an immobile horse. How come I had chosen that horse for what I had to do on that day? I suppose I felt an energetic thread to him. I must have felt in my heart, even if unconsciously, that El Dia had something to teach me. Could he lead me to understand and work through something?

I decided to leave my mind and get into my body. I closed my eyes and started to breathe in and out, then again, in and out. Suddenly my head chatter dissipated and I was able again to still my senses with the smell of the sweet grass and the mesquite trees, which emitted a very special odor, enhanced by the rays of the sun.

As I was in that space of bliss, with my eyes closed, and still on the outside of the pen, I saw – with my mind's eyes – a triangle. I turned around, this time facing the horse, and closed my eyes again. I breathed in and out, in and out. Suddenly, I saw the same triangle, but this time it was breaking into pieces. What was the triangle about?

Still wondering what the triangle meant, I stepped into the round pen. El Dia was standing immobile, waiting for me from the other side of the pen. He was standing 15 hands off the ground, with a nice body conformation, his skin shining in the hot sun, and his smell floating to me from the other side of the pen. The smell of horses calms me, and in that moment, having the scent of El Dia gently gathering in my nose, I felt home.

El Dia did not move a single part of his body. He was statuesque as he looked at me. I moved to the middle of the round pen and stopped there, slowly putting the whip, which I had carried with me, on the ground. As I looked down, I saw small pieces of mesquite mixed into the sand. The wind gently blew the earthy smell to me, through the warm air. Standing still, I became aware of something new. Something had shifted and I could now feel a strong sensation going from my heart to the heart of El Dia. It was an invisible connection, whispering to me that it would assist us in creating something together.

El Dia suddenly started to move and came toward me. This was a surprise. At the same time, I felt like I was transported on another level of consciousness and I knew what to do and when. The desire for motion propelled me to take a step and then another and the horse followed me, like we were buddies going for a stroll. His breath caressed my back as I walked in this trance-like state, yet fully aware of what was happening. El Dia's breath and presence were supporting me in doing what we were doing.

The triangle image influenced me again as my legs began to walk the image in the sand, El Dia constantly with me. When I was finished walking, I went to the center of the pen where I heard a voice telling me: "Now, you follow the horse!" I went to his back. He was now in front, and I was behind him, almost in his blind spot. He curved his neck toward me and I heard him asking: "And now what?"

"You are in charge now! What about the broken triangle you showed me before I came into the round pen?" came my answer. A contracted energy ran through my body that felt more like El Dia's state of being than mine. I was aware of the waves of information coming from his body toward mine. Then, I felt El Dia relax. He dropped his head and started to move again. All this lasted a few seconds, but it felt like an eternity, like someone had switched linear time off and we were suspended in another reality.

We were experiencing full awareness now, embedded into unconditional being; the ultimate space of co-creation. It felt like in those seconds, El Dia and I were rewriting our destiny together. He walked in front of me and, like we had done before, we were pacing a triangle.

He broke out of the form and started to walk around, apparently at random. The profoundness of his movements struck me deeply. Admiration filled my heart as I watched what was playing out in front of my eyes, with a sense of secrecy that felt like when, as a child, I had been going to church alone, just to be with God. For me, it was a sensation of belonging together, of union, of creation and co-creation; a sensation of ecstasy where all my body felt like "feel good" chemicals were running through it. There we were, a horse and a woman, in a round pen, doing apparently nothing, but having a profound experience together.

*

In that moment, I recognized that we both had something in common to work on, and with an open heart and pure intention, an obsolete form died in order to create space for something new to come. The heart connection I felt at the beginning was still there, and I was feeling as though all my senses were trying to give meaning to all that had just happened.

My awareness was wide again. The horse and I were releasing each other. What we had to do together had already happened; now we just needed time to integrate the process and to allow ourselves to function normally again. We stood for an eternal couple of seconds, in a space of complete being and oneness. To separate us at that point would have been like taking two lovers apart after reaching a space of unity with their bodies, their hearts, their energies, and their souls. It was a pity that we had to part soon after, and at the same time, necessary.

Linda's voice called to me. Almost 20 minutes had passed and she was trying to call me back to a linear time awareness. Time had passed without my awareness. I approached El Dia and thanked him for those very special moments together. My hand reached out for him and for the first time I was touching his skin. El Dia's body was hot in the sun, and very soft. He looked at me calmly and there was a short moment, as our eyes met, in which our souls connected. We were both saying thank you for what had happened between us. Thank you for holding each other's space for growing. Thank you for sharing this time together. Thank you!

Something very profound had just happened, and at the time, I did not feel like writing it down.

Four years have passed and I am very grateful to El Dia for what he did for me on that day. Only now am I able to write about it. The time since that day gave me the possibility to integrate what I needed to, to grow, and to have the strength to watch back and intellectualize what had happened on that occasion with that beautiful silent teacher. It had meant a lot for him as well. The very next day, to the disbelief of all the people watching, he danced in the round pen with Kathleen Ingram, co-creator with Linda Kohanov of the Epona Apprenticeship Program.

That day with me in the round pen, our two souls were a perfect match to work through something that was driving both of our existences. My childhood experiences had many similarities with El Dia's. As I said, El Dia had been trained to hobble. Though I did not have visible chains binding my feet, all the mental, physical, and emotional abuse by my family had the same effect as the horse's chained feet. I was not allowed to be myself. I was wrong the way I was. Everybody was very busy trying to change me to make me fit into a society that was for them, not for me. When the pressure around me became too heavy to bear, I started to dissociate from my body. In the end, my character was broken, and my spirit as well.

Maybe, while being hobbled, a horse also learns to dissociate from the body. So what apparently looks like a quiet horse is maybe just a horse who is not fully present. I had learned, like El Dia, to be a Victim of a malfunctioning society. The Victim role would also resonate with the triangle, which is used in psychology to explain the role-play of drama. Each corner represents a different role: Victim, Rescuer, Perpetrator.

El Dia and I had learned to be Victims, and the work we did together helped us both to break free from the illusion of the drama someone else wanted to become the script of our lives. El Dia showed me the way to freedom and to authentic relationship, where drama triangles are never present.

At times people make decisions for other beings – animals or children for example – without really respecting what that being would like for her/himself. The experiences in my childhood brought me to a space where I did not know any longer who I was. I just lived a life that was not mine. I was the observer of my physical presence, without being present. Most of the time, I was dissociated from my body and at times I would wake up and think: Who did this? Who said that? Then in disbelief, I would understand that it was really me who did or said something.

Although I was depressed during the majority of my childhood, my parents didn't really understand that something was wrong. It seemed to me that they never stopped and reflected about this possibility. Maybe it is like the people hobbling their horses; they think what they are doing is in the best interest of the horse, with the illusion that control is part of life.

For me, life is now about collaboration, respect, and friendship. Control is never part of my thoughts or actions. Any kind of control, whether physical, mental, emotional, or material, is like saying, "I am superior to you, therefore I will control you, whether you want it or not."

My parents, peace to their souls, still think that I am not normal. Maybe they are right. However, it does not matter to me. My husband and I have a beautiful family with four children and lots of animals, as well as many good friends. I like simple things and strive to reach self-sustainability on all levels. What is normality anyway? How does one reach it? Does it have a form? How does it taste? For me normality is a box. In this box there are also control, denial, judgment, hate, love for power, drama, scarcity, and much more.

El Dia and the other horses in my life taught me to be me, to be unique, and let my light shine, as bright as I can. The horses taught me about unity and freedom, respect, unconditional love, authentic relationship, abundance, and peace.

Sherazade

At age 20, I was able to afford my first horse, a beautiful gray Arab named Sherazade, keeping her in a livery just outside of Milan, Italy. Somehow I was able to juggle my life as a student and horse owner, working to finance both. But it got to a point at which I understood I was not ready for that horse. She was trying to teach me something I was not able to comprehend then.

Every time I went to see Sherazade, she would run toward me, her neck arched and her eyes wide open. Her mane would be flowing in the wind, her tail in the air, everything 100% sound. I loved watching her doing this display for me. She would run in circles and show me how beautiful, free, and fully into her own power she was.

After her beautiful greeting ceremony, I would bring her into the stables, compulsively clean her – even if she really didn't need it – and finally saddle and ride her.

It didn't take long before I got the feeling that something was wrong in our relationship. Soon after, she started to be lame whenever I got on her back.

In those years, I still believed that to pay the costs of a horse and then not "use" it was a waste of money. So, one day, I decided to call my grandfather Enzo, who had dedicated most of his life to breeding and racing horses. Over the years, he had become an expert in hooves and lameness. My grandfather, even though I don't feel an affinity for horse races, was a very wise man. Among other moments, I remember spending childhood days with him and his athletes, walking beautiful stallions down the stable passageways to let them dry after the races.

That warm summer day, I arrived first at the equestrian estate to see Sherazade. The trees were in their fullest beauty. The building was an old typical Italian Cascina, and Sherazade was at the back of the yard in an outside paddock. As usual, I prepared her for a ride.

When my grandfather arrived, he parked his car and walked toward us. He saw me riding Sherazade, turned around, and started to leave. I yelled after him, "And? Is there anything you can see?"

He stopped and faced me, then said, "There is nothing wrong with the horse!" He turned around again and left.

I thought, "Great, now what? There is nothing wrong with the horse. So is there maybe something wrong with me?" A voice in my head replied, "Don't worry! It is the horse. Just get rid of her." I blindly listened to this voice and gave up the horse.

Before ending the story of Sherazade, I need to mention one particular incident. Sherazade hated to have me pick up her feet and clean them, to the point that once, she managed to throw me two meters away while I was cleaning her left hind foot. This instilled in me a deep fear connected to cleaning hooves.

After Sherazade there was a gap of 10 years in which I did not come in close vicinity of horses for a prolonged time. I would go now and then to ride in different places, but I was feeling that something had changed and I was no longer interested in taking riding lessons, or jumping, or participating in events. There was something that Sherazade had left in me. Like she had been able, with her beauty and challenging character, to plant a seed into my heart, which then slowly started to blossom, and brought me to study Equine Facilitated Learning. Somehow the voice of my grandfather telling me, "There is nothing wrong with her!" became louder and louder, making me curious.

Angel Talk and the Hooves

The first time I saw Angel Talk she was five months old. She was beautiful, with Bambi eyes and the carriage of a queen. She is an Appaloosa, but I have always seen many similarities between her and Sherazade. Angel runs arching her neck, picking up her feet, and letting them touch the soil with the elegance of a prima ballerina. I am not sure who chose whom, and that does not even matter. What I know is that when I saw her I knew, with every part of my heart, that she was going to be the horse living with me.

Angel is a horse that likes to organize everything, and she let me understand she would have liked her best buddy, Rose Kisses, to come along with her. They were born on the same day and had lived together since.

In a nearby paddock there was another foal, Cowboy Justice, who had lost his mother. Finally, a year later, another filly named Silent Dream completed the herd that now works with me. They are all part of my family and constantly let me work on myself, my baggage, my shadow, my issues, and my lameness (my learned fears).

Due to my fear of cleaning hooves, early on I paid attention that the horses got used to having their hooves picked up and cleaned. All went well for many years till I started to change and the relationship the horses were offering to me shifted, always evolving, growing, changing, challenging, like a never-ending dance in harmony and trust.

The horses taught me many lessons, though there is one in particular that was very special. The horses started to refuse to have their hooves picked up and trimmed. They chased everybody away who tried to trim their hooves, but me. They would look at me with big eyes, like saying: "Do you get it?" I didn't. I wasn't able to understand till the day Angel took the process into her "hooves".

One day, I saw Angel walking slowly. I checked on her and saw a swelling just above her left hind leg hoof. I checked for injuries, but there was nothing. Then she turned around gently, now showing me her back. In that moment my awareness was brought to her right hoof. I saw that the hind corner of the hoof had split and a part of it stuck out in the direction of the other hoof. She slowly started to walk again, to show me that the part sticking out was touching the other leg.

My heart started to race, pushing my blood through my body in no time. My head spinning, I thought: "Now what? Angel is not allowing any trimmer around her feet." Unexpectedly, I heard a voice: "You are going to do this!"

Vividly remembering the scene of Sherazade throwing me two meters backward, my stomach contracted. "I cannot afford to get injured; I have family. I could get kicked in the face while pretending to be a trimmer!" Then, suddenly, peace came over me, and I heard the voice again: "Don't worry, I am going to teach you how to do it." I started to realize that this could become a great learning for me and decided to face my fears, my own lameness, trusting what Angel had told me.

So I went to get the tools for trimming. I still don't know their names, but learned quickly about their sharpness. After preparing the stables, I brought all four horses in. Then I waited for the horses to reach that space of bliss when they are eating. Everything was peaceful; the only sound came from the munching of the dried grass. Suddenly, my heartbeat jumped, making me aware that it was our time now, time for trimming.

I took the rasp and approached Angel's stable. My heart was running so fast, it felt like it would be able to escape from my body if I didn't close my mouth. I opened the door and Angel looked at me. She raised her head, and with very gentle eyes she turned around. I could not move, my fear paralyzing me, with the rasp in my bare hands and my heart still racing a Formula 1 track. Unexpectedly, Angel came backward toward me and placed her hooves in the perfect position for me to trim them. I gently moved my hand along her buttocks, down her leg, and then tried to lift the hoof with the broken side. While doing this, I had all these pictures of her kicking various farriers running through my mind.

Once again, my body relaxed and a voice said, "You know what to do, you just need to remember it!" Hearing this voice, tears started to run down my cheeks. I felt I was supposed to leave the hoof on the ground. Angel, by holding it still, would help me with the trimming. So we did. I was almost lying on the ground, behind her back legs, with my arms wrapped around them, and while she was holding the hoof on the ground, I removed the sharp edge.

I was sobbing in disbelief of everything that was happening, crying in the knowledge that she could have seriously injured me. Whereas all she did, thrice, was arch her neck in my direction, bending her head along her body, like trying to reach and tell me with her gentle eyes, "Trust me, I have asked you to do this; I will not hurt you!"

Now my tears were of joy, mixed with disbelief and love; love for a creature who injured herself to help me improve our relationship. To develop *trust* in a horse relationship, like in any other relationship, is a giant step forward! Angel helped me to trust her and to understand that when she or one of the other three needed anything, they would be able to let me know. Then, somehow, we would find a solution together.

This is the biggest achievement I could have ever dreamed about in the relationship with my horses – trust that is driven by the respect for each other and the capabilities that the other has to offer. The trust that brings us to listen to the other, then listen again, and then act.

Almost two years have passed since that day, during which I have trimmed their hooves on many other occasions, with Angel giving me more lessons in trimming. She even taught a master trimmer some lessons. It is just phenomenal how she knows all that she knows, and how generous her spirit is. Now I understand what my Grandfather Enzo was meaning when he said: "There is nothing wrong with the horse!" Angel taught me that horses will even harm themselves, if it is necessary to make us listen. Such is their commitment to teaching humans!

Thus it is in our hands to respond to their teaching. We need to be ready to face what the horses are mirroring back to us. Their lessons can be difficult to accept, because our fears, stored deep in our body, are our biggest enemies.

Angel helped me to be in the present moment during the trimming process. This was essential to calibrate the flow of information between her and myself to a point where I could instantly interpret her movements – even twitches of her muscles – and her emotions. We were in perfect harmony, like a flame in the wind and its mirror image.

Please note: If you like to try out the horse-guided hoof trimming, be aware that it is risky. And protect your hands! After my first time, my hands were covered in blood, as I didn't realize how sharp the trimming tools are. Nowadays, I trim all four horses when they need it. They are responsible for the trimming; I just follow their instructions. We are on a path of open learning.

Trust the Horse

Horses are for me master teachers and consensual companions in growth. Our relationships are based on listening and trusting. Respect for the other is one of the basic values we have, as well as integrity and purity of intent, unconditional love, and freedom. We live and act as an equine-human herd. We are the change.

Meanwhile, many people have become interested in our way of being. We have connected with our nomadic roots and are traveling between Africa and Europe to share with others. Our sharing brings peace to the minds of people, and spreads warmth in their hearts. They regain their powers and connect with their paradise on earth.

Our horse-human herd keeps on growing and is setting good foundations for the times to come. Life is beautiful and abundant, and horses are, as they have always been, at our side in these times of growth; times in which humanity is asked to make a leap in consciousness. The path is an easy one and many people are now holding hands to help each other. Just trust the horse, she or he will show you the way!

Angel Talk

To my companion Karsten, for being my Hero and Angel on earth; my children: Alexander, Edoardo, Leonardo, and Lorenzo, for continually challenging me to find different ways of doing things; to Kathleen Ingram for being such a great teacher, mentor, and trusted sister; and to the many horses, spirits, and people, visible and invisible, who have been at my side on this earthly path, I thank you from the depths of my heart.

❋

About
Vanessa Malvicini

Vanessa feels she is a horse among a herd, a beautiful grey mare. For the past nine years, she has dedicated her life to the horses: to study them, to be with them and, ultimately, to work with them in a consensual way.

Vanessa's approach, which she developed together with the horses living with her, offers the possibility to experience working with horses at liberty, in their fullest expression. Likewise, participants in her programs will be able to express themselves to the fullest, in a safe environment, where emotions are used as information, the same way the horses do it. Their wild side holds space for the wild side of humans, enabling them to break free again from the expectations of society and to reach that sense of peace and stillness that is a birthright to us. This process allows people to get to know themselves and helps them to create and be in a relationship in freedom.

When people ask whether Vanessa is a horse whisperer, she replies that she is a Horse Priestess. Her work isn't about training horses; it is about personal development at the side of the horses. Her main teachers are the Horses, the Spirits, and the Ancestors. Vanessa works with no structure and loves to share her passion for an easy and abundant life. Vanessa holds a vision of a time in which women will dance and sing together and nurture each other.

While building with her family their own little country retreat, the

Appaloosa Horse Farm south of Cape Town, South Africa, she started to discover her true self. Vanessa is still in constant personal development and strives to be on the path to self-sufficiency, inside and outside. She shares her time between family, researches, personal development, and work, both in South Africa and Europe, holding workshops in English, German, and Italian. She is an Epona Approved Instructor/Facilitator and the core of her work is based on the teachings of Linda Kohanov and Kathleen Ingram. The Hearth Flame Grail Mare Mystery School component of Vanessa's work is based on The Priest/ess Process™, created by Nicole Christine and her initiatory work with Nicole and Robbie Nelson.

Vanessa is an NLP Master Practitioner and a Relationship, Spiritual, and Life Coach. She holds degrees in Ericksonian Hypnotherapy and Energy Resourcing. Currently, she is alining with the Divine Creation High Priestess energies, with Cayelin K Castell holding her hand.

For more information about Vanessa and her work, visit www. iCavalli.co.za, email Vanessa@Malvicini.org, or call the Appaloosa Horse Farm in Noordhoek, South Africa: Tel. +27 73 336 35 36.

Honoring the Wisdom of the Horse: The Four Archetypes of Human/Horse Relationship

By Juli Lynch

For the past forty years, my life has been blessed with the presence of horses. My fascination with horses, their personalities, and behavior parallel my fascination with the personalities and behaviors of people who work, ride, show, and love them. I believe that human personality and resulting behaviors are the manifestation of evolving archetypes that have been present since homo sapiens have been in relationship with one another. Each of us carries a "blueprint" or a "program" of personality that is a reflection of these archetypes.

Horses know these archetypes of our personalities and recognize them perhaps better than we do ourselves. As teachers, their behavior – not always, but often – is a response to specific energetic qualities of each archetype and how we manifest them in their presence. This is the story of the archetypes of personality that I've discovered and suggest in my work with people and horses.

Allow me to "hand over the reins" and the telling of this particular story of a horse, the humans in his life, and the archetypes of those humans to what I've imagined as this horse's perspective.

Horse Speaks

The ancient oral traditions of the Mayan civilization, sacred Tibetan scripture, as well as the teachings of native culture – the Hopi, the Lakota, the Navajo – all speak of a time when interspecies connection and communication will bring the relationship between humans and horses into harmony. The teachings say that the time is now and that humans know of this way because humans lived this harmony in the past – at a time when people were more connected to nature and moved in balance with the wisdom of the herd. In tribal times, the herd viewed humans as the Keepers, Warriors, Healers, and Shaman.

These archetypes still exist today, yet manifest with little conscious awareness from the human. They emerge when you are with us – the way you think of us, see us, talk to us, believe in us, care for us, ride us – the way you are in relationship with us. This is a story of my relationships with humans and the four archetypes.

The Keeper

Her smell reminded me of when I was still at my mother's side. That same fragrance would erupt after the long, clear nights that snatched our breaths from us and left icicles on our chins. I would sense it as we stood warming ourselves beneath the lengthening light of each rising sun. I'd release this odor as my lips wrestled with a dried clump of last year's clover. If I was patient and persistence – wriggling my nose to dig down deeper – I'd come upon a succulent sprig of new spring clover, and that perfume – the smell of sweet dirt drunk on the water of snow melt – would fill my nostrils and make my head dizzy.

She smelled of muzzled clover – a fragrance that arrived before she did on the breeze that would sneak down the aisle when the big opening in the barn showed us the outside. Sometimes I'd press my cheek to the bars to catch a glimpse of blue sky beyond the big opening. Once I smelled her arrival, I'd watch. First I'd see her boots – moving unaffected by pain or age – always in a rhythm of one-two-one-two. As her knees, hips, and waist came into view I'd hold my breath in anticipation of her eyes. But first I'd see the mouth – cautious and pinched as if holding in secret thoughts too complex to place in the care of words – and the nose, so tight and restrained, suspicious of the potential of full breath. And then the eyes – always they were the same – eyes of remembrance and concern, distantly thoughtful, separate from the body, as if not seeing an immediate world in front of them, but rather a world more complex, more intense, more demanding and draining.

I would snort a greeting – a "hello, so you've arrived." But without notice or acknowledgment, she'd just stand before me. I'd fill my nostrils with her scent and feel my heart reach, as if a hand, to touch what would not be there – warmth, engagement, a synchronization of blood pulsing in harmonious joy at this reunion. It was always out of reach, a heart pulled back, hidden and protected by intellect, reason, and purpose. I exhaled disappointment. She wouldn't notice. I would resist the urge to sniff, to nuzzle. I knew this was neither friend nor foe – neither provider nor predator. This was simply someone not seeing me, and in not seeing there would be no connection.

She'd reach forward and I'd hear the clank of metal moving with effort. Light would come suddenly into my box, tossed into my space, splattering the varnished walls. I'd wince at the suddenness of the light; its adamant entrance into my world of ebony shadows.

"Come on," she would say, as she would turn to step into the light. A firm tug behind my ears and across my nose would always instill an instinct to pull back, but stronger memories suggested a wiser choice. I would step forward.

"Stand," would come from her mouth, and I knew what was next. It was always the same. A precise ritual of preparation: First my feet – left front, left rear, right front, right rear; next, the scratchy thing beneath my mane, across my shoulder, down and around my belly, up and over my hip, and off the end of my tail; always one side, then the other. Then came the soft thing; it would make me lick and chew and exhale slowly, always one side, then the other.

Sometimes she would speak to nobody in particular, in a matter-of-fact tone. "Gotta call the farrier. Why aren't they blanketing you at night? I have to remember to order supplements." My tail was always last, getting the most attention. Her fingers would rake slowly, pausing at the tangles, reversing their intention to morph into knots. She never recognized my contentment and appreciation of this routine.

If we had any semblance of a relationship – an agreement of mutuality – perhaps it was around my willingness to stand still, and her willingness to rub and shine my coat so that even I noticed its reflection in the aisle windows. Unfortunately, when she put herself on my back, the relationship withered. I'd move to the right or the left, posing the question, "Is this what you want?" My response to her pressure yielded no release from her. More often than not the reply was, "No." The bit would speak to me the language of her frustration, the pulling and harsh jabs translating as dissatisfaction and disappointment. My blood pumped adrenaline and my mind warned, "Keep trying."

Some days the release did come and I'd sigh heavily as she slapped my neck, "Good job." But most days we struggled to find a common language. Over time I noticed that her eyes were becoming more and more distant, distracted, and full of disdain. Our rides began to end with her abrupt dismount and departure – the apple treat forgotten.

Dear Cousin;

The divorce has gotten ugly, but what's worse is my showing this season is even uglier. The Williamson's are winning everything and taking home all the big money. I'm not taking anything home. Apparently, they are paying some big time trainer big bucks to work their horses every day. Their horses know their job in the show arena and can win with those idiots just holding on for dear life. Anyway I'm not writing you to complain. I'm writing to see if you want my horse. You remember him – the big Bay. When I bought him I thought he had everything – breeding, ability, attitude, and looks. We had a winning record for awhile. Maybe it is me – the divorce and all – but he and I are not getting along. Maybe he'd do better for you. So I'm asking you to take him so I can find something else to ride and show. Let me know asap. I'm ready to send him immediately. Oh, by the way, his coat is immaculate. I groom it every day, spending at least an hour on it. His tail is gorgeous. See if you can find the time to maybe groom him once or twice a month. I know you.

Sincerely, Your "Little Cousin"

Dawn arrived misty eyed. Dew streamed like teardrops down the barred windows of my box stall. That day I heard her before I smelled her. Her boots moved in a quicker rhythm of one-two-one-two. For the last time I pressed my cheek to the bars to watch her approach. Her mouth came into view revealing a softness I'd never seen. She slid the metal and stepped into my box. I remember to this day how she looked me in the eye, and before she spoke I knew I was leaving.

"You're going to go work with someone that won't be as patient as I am. Someone who will insist you work to your ability. I don't know why you and I don't get along. I've given you everything. Behave yourself. I don't want you coming back." She rested her hand on my neck as she spoke these words. I wanted to lean into her, to turn my head and nuzzle her shoulder. I didn't. I stood still, looking forward, waiting for her to leave. When she did, I exhaled with a deep, low grunt and watched through the bars as she walked away.

In tribal times the Keeper "kept" our lineage pure. The Keeper selected us for qualities eminent to the tribe's survival – workhorse, warhorse, sure-footed horse, pack horse. The Keeper knew that the herd's freedom to move, freedom to roam, and freedom to run kept legs swift, necks powerful, and spines strong.

Today the Keeper is the horseperson who strives for the order of all things related to us – all things exacting in our pedigree, our care, our looks, and our performance. We are well "kept", but not in a natural state. We are separate – a status symbol, owned, showed, and sold, or left to spend our days in small boxes away from any kind of herd or emotional engagement with humans.

The Warrior

I remember those first few mornings. Dawn would slip beneath the shade of darkness, pushing pinkish-orange pastels across the horizon. As the night shadows disappeared my pasture mates appeared. Uninspired by the delicate unfolding of a new day, they'd stand, hips cocked and snoring, oblivious to my exuberance. Dawn docsn't paint the walls of a 12 x 12 box stall. The open field gave me my own private showing.

He smelled of smoking tobacco, sharp and bitter, the scent floated in with the breeze that tussled my mane. His movements werc big and bold, his boots always hurried, marching, purposeful – half running, half skipping. He'd pause at the gate and I'd watch him, curious.

"I need a Camel," he'd say. Reaching into his shirt pocket the crackle of a little square box brought us all to attention – perhaps a treat would emerge. Instead, another cigarette would replace the one smoldering to a snub on the edge of his lip. The smoke would curl from his mouth upward, hiding, then revealing his eyes; eyes that cried little and laughed often; eyes that could bore an intensity of expectation into you with little room for negotiation. The same eyes that, with a sparkle and a wink, would say, "Let's do something wild and reckless today."

In the arena we were intense, unpredictable, yet connected. The crowds loved us and stood to cheer our performances. Our intention was synchronized, our focus singular. He allowed and I responded. He requested and I agreed. He'd hesitate and I'd decide.

I remember the show where the air was thick with anticipation. The smoke from his Camel hung like a shroud, draped off our shoulders, heavy and confining. The usual lightness of his touch on the reins hung heavy too. I could feel the dry swallow of his anxious energy all the way down my spine. "This is the big one ole boy," he said through his cigarette. "We get one chance here. Let's knock em' dead."

His hips shifted with subtle deft – my cue to move out of the smoke and toward the gate that opened into the arena. My foot dropped into dirt too deep for comfort, catching me ever so slightly so that I had to jerk my knees in order to make forward progress. He asked me a little stronger for a 3-beat gait. Feeling the bit drop against my tongue and rotate forward,

I lowered my head and obliged. I released my hocks back and down and felt my back lift to meet the subtle requests of his seat.

Then I felt the twist to the left as my hind leg planted, and an uncoiling to the right that couldn't be completed. It was as if a hand held my leg as the rest of me was pushed off a cliff, leaving the leg to take the force of my shear weight. I heard the tear inside my head as it rushed up the back of my cannon bone to my hock. My breath exploded from me in audible anguish. My nostrils reclaimed my breath in a desperate attempt to hold the moment still – to halt its unfolding and keep it from being real.

He was off me and yelling to someone, stroking my neck, "It's ok boy, thata boy. We had a bad turn. Blasted footing. It will be okay buddy." His words shook with unsteady expression; his hands stroked the fear rippling down my spine, but did nothing to dissipate it. His shallow, raspy, and rapid breath matched my own, amplifying our shared despair.

He urged me forward with a cluck of his tongue. I touched my hoof to the ground and snatched it back, reluctant to trust my weight upon it. At the gate, eyes met mine with breaths held, hands reached out to pat my neck, shoulders, back, and haunches. Voices offered words of comfort, but the strain of uncertainty was apparent. As I moved away from the crowd, the electricity in the air turned sullen and still. I heard no cheering, no laughter. I knew I wouldn't be back.

Dearest Sis,

I was wondering if you would have room for one more horse? That big Bay I've been showing got hurt and will be out of commission – maybe forever. I don't have time to give him the care he needs and I know you love to rehab horses and you are a lot better at it than I am. You have the patience. He is a great horse. We were really kickin' it up – winning everything. He loved to show and he and I made a great team. I can bring him down Saturday. Plan on keeping him as long as you want. Maybe he could become one of those therapy horses you work with. The vets aren't too confident that he'll show again. I could cry when I think of the pain he is enduring. He is so tough. He has a big heart and a can-do attitude. He's not a quitter and will work as hard as you do to get better. I hope this letter finds you feeling well. It will be good to see you again. I know I stay away too long.

Your Big Brother

The Warrior gave us the courage to trust the tribe, the willingness to leave the herd, the respect to die with honor. The Warrior knew that partnership was the only way to build an enduring relationship with us. The Warrior

knew that to sit upon our backs was the greatest honor the herd could bestow – the most profound expression of trust between predator and prey. When we grew old or injured we were respected and honored and given to the children to ride.

Today the Warrior still lives for the thrill and exhilaration of celebrating our power and speed. Upon our back the Warrior is at home waiting for the next challenge or opportunity to fly like the wind. Just as quickly, the Warrior will become uninterested when we are perceived as having nothing left to offer. A younger, healthier, or faster horse will be chosen over us, and we will be seen as broken down or useless – our purpose served.

The Healer

I remember the days melting into night, but I don't remember what unfolded around me as the hours passed. Each breath was cut short by the stab of pain in my leg. Each shift of weight I'd attempt in order to seek comfort was limited to a narrow range of options. Discomfort moved across my body like the chilling winds of the late autumn days of which I was vaguely aware.

Her smell caused my nostrils to crinkle then flare into a long exhale that relaxed me. When she moved in close I could smell it on her hands that seemed to arrive before the rest of her – always reaching out, touching me, rubbing me, moving along my spine, across my rump, down my legs.

She would talk in rhythm with her hands, "There, there, now, that's better isn't it? Ooooo," she'd coo, "How's that today?" I'd respond with a sigh and slight resignation, because I was uncomfortable. She'd work on my leg – gently at first, flexing my ankle, asking my hock to fold and release. I'd close my eyes and lull as she'd rest her hand on my rump and hum a melancholy melody, reassuring me that I would be fine. Her eyes often looked beyond me in the moment and seemed to tap a deeper pool of wisdom that allowed her to know what I needed. I felt safe with her, able to relax into my vulnerability and know that she would protect me.

Over time, however, I began to feel consumed by her, and as time progressed there were days I did not look forward to her touch. I was healing and did not need as much care as she needed to give me. On these days she'd arrive with her hands ready to reach for me and I'd instinctively turn away. She'd respond with a treat from her pocket. Standing with my hindquarters to her, I'd glance over my shoulder, my mouth salivating. Reluctantly I'd turn, the treat overpowering my instinct to ignore her.

I began to long for a lope across a plush pasture or a grand roll in the mud. She did not ride me – she could have – my leg yearned to be stretched at a trot and a canter. I would have liked that. Instead she fussed over me. I was outside, but in a confined space – because of her inability to trust my own self-care instincts. I wanted to lean my withers into the warm muzzle of a nibbling herd mate.

Her generosity toward me was unconditional. But over time, she needed to heal me more then I needed healing. As I became healthier I noticed a sad quality to her eyes that hadn't been present when I first came to her. I realized that she was no longer healing me. She was healing herself, and her daily rituals of ointments and oils on my body were reflective of the healing she wished for herself.

During that time she began to change. Her once strong hands moved with diminishing purpose, pausing longer and retiring sooner. There were days when she would not work on me at all. She'd bring a chair and sit with me. I'd watch her get lost in the tracking of a maple leaf skipping across the gravel, or she'd hum softly to me, a voice sad and worn with the effort of breath. I sensed a diminishing light, a resignation of sorts, an acceptance of all things coming and going. When she did touch me she'd often just lean against my shoulder and breathe. I'd lean back, holding her up. She'd drop her forehead to my mane. I'd feel her tears along my crest, droplets of grief.

My dearest friend on this earth,

As you know the lump that began as a small acorn has grown to the size of the apples in the orchard. It is spreading throughout my body. I'm being well cared for and have probably been given more time than expected. I have a favor to ask. Can you take the Bay I've been rehabbing? He is almost 100% now, but will need supportive care for his injury. I know you have the space and I know you will see his wisdom and grandeur. He has given me so much through this ordeal. He has a heart of gold. I could see him becoming a horse who works with the kids you bring to the ranch. When you see his eyes you will know. He is special. I will wait to hear from you and pray that this will work out.

With deepest gratitude

The day dawned gray and foreboding the last time I ever saw her. The clouds gathered above my paddock in layers – moving and rearranging themselves as if unsettled and uncertain whether to rain or snow. She came to me slowly. Her scent no longer arrived with her hands. Instead her sadness arrived, matching the mood of the sky.

"I hope this weather holds," she said. "Winter wants us bad now doesn't it?" She stood for the longest time just looking at me. I held her gaze and my heart swelled. She stepped into my paddock and pulled my neck to her cheek. "I love you big Bay. I'll miss you." This time I did not pull away. I sighed and lowered my head in gratitude for all she had done for me, and acceptance for all she didn't understand.

The Healer was there in tribal times to lay a hand on our wounds, to assist as our foals struggled to arrive, and to ease us into our last breaths. The Healer worked in harmony with the gifts of the earth – the plants, the waters, the rocks, and the roots. The Healer understood that healing came through time and patience – through causing no further harm, while allowing the herd's own way of healing to be honored and allowed.

Today as humans come into harmony with the herd, the Healer is understanding better our need to heal through natural means – through time and effort and gentler ways of interacting with our bodies. The resources at the Healer's disposal are significant, and therefore, at times, too much. The Healers of today must remember that the environment that surrounds any healing is as crucial as the cure.

The Shaman

I remember those first mornings. Dawn came to me as a nudge on my neck, the quick flick of a muzzle, soft but insistent. My eyelids flickered as sleep gave way to awareness. Two deep set eyes framed by a white forehead and cheekbones greeted me. Her soft, throaty nicker cued a return nicker from me. I tossed my head and she lifted her neck and dropped her nose to her chest, her shoulder bumping mine.

Together we waited, our breaths silver clouds hanging low on our nostrils. The crunch and squeak of snow under foot would announce his arrival. I would smell him, the rich, aromatic scent of roasted earth in a mug he carried cupped in his bare palm, the rough, red muscled flesh insulation enough for him on cold winter dawns. Steam would hover above the mug as if avoiding the inevitability of annihilation in air too dry and cold to welcome anything warm. His breath hovered too, just beyond his mouth, leaving ice tendrils on a chin of gray and brown whiskers. His nostrils would pause mid-breath as if sniffing the wind.

At times he'd turn as if listening to the stories only the wind could tell. His eyes matched the winter sky – cobalt blue – a stark contrast to his weathered cheeks and crevassed brow, like two pools of motionless water sunk into sun-baked bedrock. His eyes harbored a story of lessons learned and resolve, of tragedy and loss that brings a quieting to the soul, of tears wept at full moons with gaped mouth and gulping grief. And yet there was peace, an acceptance of all that ultimately unfolds, with gratitude directed toward us. Had horses been his Savior?

He said little, but spoke volumes to us. With the lift of his chin he could direct one of us to move away. With the tilt of his head one of us would come to him. With the exhale of his breath we all would gather at the gate and step back when he nodded his head. When he arrived with his saddle we'd jockey for position. "Choose me," we'd nicker.

When I was chosen, we'd ride up to the meadows, over to the forest, down the lanes, and along the rocky, winding trails. Hours later he'd deliver me back to the herd, but not without offering a wedge of apple or snip of carrot and a gentle brush on the neck to say, "Thank you."

One morning I heard the boy before I saw him, a strange whirring sound, the low hum of a small motor. We all looked up in unison from our hay, mouths full, dripping with green juice and half torn stems.

The boy appeared initially as a tiny speck of silver accompanied by the growing sound of the whirring motor. He walked beside the boy, who appeared to be approaching us in a moving chair! He sipped his mug of steaming coffee and spoke softly to the boy as they approached. When they arrived at the gate we were all there to greet them, curious, cautious, and relieved that the boy was friend not foe.

With the lift of his chin he sent the herd away. As I turned to leave he called out my name and tilted his head as an invitation to join the two of them. Feeling curious, I moved toward the gate. He opened the gate and brought me to stand above the boy. A long inhale revealed the smells of soap and salt and something sweet like peppermint. The boy's eyes grew large, his head tilted back, and his mouth opened, a silent cry of alarm. I sensed this and took a step back.

He spoke with the boy, reassuring him, and then spoke to me, "Nice and easy there big guy – he's a little afraid of you – you're awful big." I dropped my head and slowly inched my nose forward. My nostrils quivered as I tried to be still, but still reach out to him. I held my breath, fearing my exhalation would be too much and scare him. Tiny fingers, no larger than the bloated worms that emerged from the dirt after the rain, inched forward on the tray that hid his lap. Like a spider, his fingers walked along the tray, paused at the edge, and then began to walk up my lip to the bridge between my nostrils.

The boy pressed his fingers into my nose, causing me to release my breath, a poof of air that lifted the blond bangs on his forehead. He pulled his fingers away, tilted his head back, and laughed a silent laugh that could be felt all the way back to the herd.

As I watched them leave, the herd came to join me, nuzzling me and sniffing me, trying to learn the story of this odd encounter. As we all watched, the boy whirred away in his chair. The winter clouds that had kept us blanketed for days began to pull back, introducing sheets of blue sky and a warming sun. We knew that this was the promise of a returning spring and the hint of a not too distant summer.

The Shaman whispered what others could not hear. They understood the connection of that not seen – of that only felt or sensed or suggested. The Shaman saw the flick of our ears, the shift of our eyes, the swish of our tails, and knew its meaning, knew its message. The Shaman knew our souls and honored those young and old. He sought us out for wisdom and sat in counsel with us to better learn our ways. He brought to us those who needed to heal and knew that a muzzle upon a brow, or a breath upon a forehead brought blessings of divine proportions.

The Shaman is again emerging, as the harmonic bond between humans and horses is discovered. The Shaman is the balance of the other three archetypes: Keeper, Healer, and Warrior. The Shaman is able to tap into the energy of each archetype, understanding the value of all three relationships when in balance. The Shaman exists as potential for all humans who honor the wisdom of the horse – the language by which we connect with all humans.

I know of you and your way of being before your hand reaches for the gate latch. I know your way of being as you approach me, as you touch me, halter me, lead me, tie me, brush me, saddle me, and ride me. I also know that at this time many of the human/horse relationships are out of balance, lacking the harmony that is so possible between us.

Keeper: Do not seek out dominance over us, but rather "allow" a dance of give and take. Understand how important it is for us to be connected to a herd – to "allow" us to be horses.

Warrior: Avoid exploiting us as a means to your end; instead join us in partnership so that we can be brilliant together.

Healer: Balance your care without disabling us with overprotection and restrictions so we become empowered with your healing wisdom.

Shaman: Do not keep your understanding of connection a secret. Share it and teach it to the children so that the next generation of horse people can forge a relationship that gives both our species the optimal chance to survive.

Human Speaks

What archetype do you manifest with the horses in your life? With the people in your life? The path of relationship with our horses closely parallels the path of relationship with the humans in our lives. Self-discovery of who we are and the subsequent changes in ways of being is now in our destiny. Our horses are showing up one by one to show us the way to relationships of balance, harmony, respect, and love. If we are willing to "give them the reins," they will show us the way.

Finnegan

To Chris my best friend and husband – my heart swells with gratitude for the unconditional love and support you give me – especially when I tell you I've acquired yet another horse! To my mother who first placed my feet in the stirrups and my hands on the reins – and now the pen in my hand – the depth of love I feel for you brings tears to my eyes. To all my four legged teachers past, present, and future, I am blessed, honored, and in awe of all you have taught me.

About
Juli Lynch

Juli can't remember a time when horses were not a part of her life. Her mother had horses as a young woman and instilled in Juli a love of them at a young age. She began showing at an early age. In college Juli became a riding instructor/trainer and took up the equine sport of eventing.

After college, Juli entered the hunter/jumpers show circuit. She rode and showed the horse of her dreams, Zhivago, a Warmblood gelding. The

Zhivago with Juli

two of them graced the hunter circuit, winning many equitation divisions. Zhivago is the horse that speaks to Juli in her dreams. and speaks in her stories.

Juli's reputation as an accomplished ultra distance runner gave her the opportunity to join a team of U.S. Navy SEALS to do an epic race across Patagonia, Argentina – called the Raid Gaulois. One section of the race required the teams to spend three days on horseback. A woman named Bonnie Mielke, one of the most experienced endurance riders in America, lived down the road from Juli. The first time Juli showed up at Bonnie's to learn about endurance riding, Bonnie threw her on one of her Arab endurance horses and took off down the trail. Juli held on for dear life through the twists and turns and galloping speeds. Juli didn't fall off and Bonnie invited her back. This turned into a decade-long opportunity to ride and race Bonnie's horses.

In 2006, Juli studied with Linda Kohanov, author of *The Tao of Equus* and founder of the Epona Approach. Linda gave her a gift no other riding instructor or trainer ever had – the gift to understand horses at a soul level – energetically and spiritually. During that time a Trekenar mare named Lizzy and a Quarterhorse named Finnegan – both trained in dressage – became Juli's newest horse teachers.

Today, Juli is an Advanced Approved Epona instructor, and both Lizzy and Finn work as partners with Juli in her equine assisted personal and professional development programs.

Juli has a doctorate in organizational and human development from the Fielding Graduate Institute. She has worked with business managers, leaders, and teams over the past 15 years as a consultant and executive coach. Today Juli is co-founder of epala® (Equine Partnerships for Authenticity, Learning and Awareness) an equine assisted personal and professional development program that combines Juli's business as a personal life coach and professional executive coach along with her qualification as an Advanced Epona instructor. Juli also conducts Who Am I with My Horse® workshops, where she works with both horses and humans and their personality archetypes.

You can find Juli at her home in the woods of Northern Wisconsin with her husband – riding or playing with her horses (Lizzy, Finnegan, Feather, and LG) or running in the woods with her dogs Abby and Amber.

For more information, email julilynch@gmail.com or visit www.epala.org

Author Contact Information

Linda-Ann Bowling	www.unbridlinghumanpotential.com
Rachel Dexheimer	www.equispire.com
Juli Lynch	www.epala.org
Vanessa Malvicini	www. iCavalli.co.za
Mary Elizabeth Meyers	www.harmonicriding.com
Caroline Rider	www.riderhorsemanship.com
Helen Amanda Russell	www.horsepatter.com
Debra A. Saum	www.dcbrasaum.com
Sandra Wallin	www.chironsway.com
Birgit Weskamp	www.horseworldjourneys.com

Editor Contact Information

Kathy Pike	www.coachingwithhorses.com
Marilyn Schwader	www.clarityofvision.com

For more information, visit
www.HorseAsTeacher.com